FRANKLIN'S LOST SHIP

THE HISTORIC DISCOVERY OF
HMS *EREBUS*

JOHN GEIGER AND ALANNA MITCHELL

FRANKLIN'S LOST SHIP

THE HISTORIC DISCOVERY OF
HMS *EREBUS*

WITH A FOREWORD BY THE HON. LEONA AGLUKKAQ

HarperCollins*PublishersLtd*

Published by HarperCollins Publishers Ltd

First edition

The authors thank all of the partners in the Victoria Strait Expedition for their contributions to this book, in particular the staff of Parks Canada, Government of Nunavut, Fisheries and Oceans Canada, and Defence Research Development Canada, who provided valuable comments. Thank you also to *Canadian Geographic* staff, including Aaron Kylie, Tyrone Burke and Jessica Finn, and to the team at HarperCollins.

HarperCollins books may be purchased for educational, business, or sales promotional use through our Special Markets Department.

HarperCollins Publishers Ltd
2 Bloor Street East, 20th Floor
Toronto, Ontario, Canada
M4W 1A8

www.harpercollins.ca

Library and Archives Canada Cataloguing in Publication information is available

ISBN 978-1-44344-417-0

Printed and bound in the United States

QG 9 8 7 6 5 4 3 2 1

To Alvaro Geiger and Sebastian Geiger

CONTENTS

Flanked by the Canadian Hydrographic Service boats *Gannet* and *Kinglett*, Parks Canada's *Investigator* makes a celebratory pass of the Canadian Coast Guard icebreaker *Sir Wilfrid Laurier*. Looking on from the bridge of the *Laurier*, Captain Bill Noon congratulated "Harris Squadron," named for archaeologist Ryan Harris, whose resolve to find *Erebus* was unwavering.

FOREWORD

I N T H E M O S T R E M O T E R E G I O N S of the Canadian Arctic, and amid ocean swells and sub-zero temperatures, the crew of the ship worked tirelessly, ever hoping to succeed in their search of the waters of the Northwest Passage. After hundreds of hours spent searching unsuccessfully, the fruitlessness of such an effort began to sink in. Then, as suddenly as an Arctic blizzard appears, a mystery of more than a century and a half was finally solved.

As an image of one of the two lost Franklin expedition ships emerged on sonar to the elation of the search team, everyone who had dedicated so much of their lives to the search at once knew their efforts had paid off. In a matter of minutes, our Inuit oral history had been validated, the elders and historians who kept the oral traditions alive were heroes and the importance of Inuit in the Canadian story was cemented. No doubt this simple image of a wreck on the bottom of the ocean had forever changed the North and, indeed, our entire country.

Turn the clock back 170 years: on May 19, 1845, the Royal Navy's HMS *Erebus* and HMS *Terror* departed England on a much-heralded Arctic expedition in search of the Northwest Passage, under the command of Sir John Franklin, with Captain Francis Rawdon Crozier second-in-command. The expedition's two ships with 129 officers and crew were last seen by European whalers as both ships entered Baffin Bay in late July 1845. This is where the Franklin mystery first began.

Since that time, many expeditions were sent to the Canadian Arctic in an attempt to learn the fate of Sir John Franklin's expedition and uncover the secrets of the North.

With a concerted effort for close to a decade, the Government of Canada, working closely with many devoted partners and utilizing Inuit traditional knowledge, has continued this search, pursuing and sharing a passion for the raw beauty and history of Canada's Arctic. To build on this momentum, for the 2014 search we brought together the largest contingent of search partners ever. In September 2014, the efforts of this dedicated team paid off with the incredible discovery and identification of Franklin's flagship, *Erebus*. Discovering the final resting place of *Erebus* is the most significant step yet toward solving one of the world's greatest maritime mysteries, capturing the imagination of a nation and igniting worldwide attention.

As the Right Honourable Stephen Harper, prime minister of Canada, noted, the discovery of *Erebus* was "truly a historic moment for Canada. Franklin's ships are an important part of Canadian history given that his expeditions, which took place nearly two hundred years ago, laid the foundations of Canada's Arctic sovereignty."

While these search efforts have greatly contributed to an important chapter in the history of our country, they have also increased our knowledge of one of the world's most remote and unforgiving places.

It is truly a story of Inuit traditional knowledge, blended with historical documents and modern-day technology. But it is also a story of perseverance, teamwork and the Canadian spirit.

Since 2008, the Government of Canada has conducted six major searches for the lost Franklin ships, working closely with our partners, painstakingly covering many hundreds of square kilometres of the Arctic seabed. Remarkably, by the time the team began their search in 2014, over 1,200 square kilometres of the Arctic seabed—the equivalent to over 2,200 football fields—had been newly surveyed and charted as part of these search efforts.

The discovery of the holy grail of shipwrecks was not done alone. This work is truly the result of partnerships and united passion for the Arctic.

Local Inuit played a key role in the locating of *Erebus*, as past ancestors had many recollections of seeing the two ships and their officers and men and had shared their observations with nineteenth-century rescue expeditions. These stories were then recorded and published, but they were also transmitted through oral history. All of these traditional accounts kept the story of Franklin alive and contributed immensely to the discovery of the wreck, helping focus efforts in the greatly debated southern search location. I know firsthand how important traditional knowledge of the land and water is. It informs our history and shapes our daily lives, helping us look forward as our elders pass this knowledge on to every new generation. I have great pride in knowing this discovery will help Canadians learn how valuable Inuit traditional knowledge is.

In addition, the discovery would not have happened without the integral help of so many other partners, each of whom brought resources, knowledge, expertise, dedication and technology. Government partners for the 2014 Victoria Strait Expedition included Parks Canada, Fisheries and Oceans Canada (the Canadian Coast Guard and Canadian Hydrographic Service), the Royal Canadian Navy, Defence Research and Development Canada, Environment Canada (including the Canadian Ice Service), and the Canadian Space Agency, as well as the governments of Nunavut and the United Kingdom. We were also proud to work with private and non-profit partners, including the Arctic Research Foundation, and The Royal Canadian Geographical Society, who additionally brought in The W. Garfield Weston Foundation, Shell Canada and One Ocean Expeditions as partners.

Canada's Arctic is a cornerstone of our national identity. Beyond its symbolic significance, the Arctic is of vital importance to our continued growth as a nation and on many critical fronts, including foreign affairs, our sovereignty, northern security, the environment, culture and the economy. Through the pursuit of common interests in the Arctic, collectively we are standing up for Canada, providing significant benefits to Canadians and helping to advance important northern goals.

Safety and security are critical to the North with the ever-growing fascination to visit this unique place. Through marine charting and other research, each expedition contributes to making Canada's Arctic both safer and more secure. To date, the marine charting associated with this work has created a new navigational route, reducing vessel transit time by approximately seven hours around the western shore of King William Island.

Supporting our Arctic communities requires broad collaboration. Many aspects of the Franklin project celebrate northern history and culture, and contribute to the sustainability of northern communities in tangible ways. Many of our partners work with northern communities to meet local needs, whether through sharing research vessels, supporting scientific research and studies, or the operation of Arctic cruises, generating significant revenues for local communities.

The Franklin research continues to allow Canadians across the country and people from around the world to learn about and enjoy the mysteries of the Franklin expedition. I welcome the opportunity to continue working with our partners into the future so that Canadians can personally connect with and be inspired by this remarkable story as it continues to unfold. As I write this foreword, the Government of Canada plans for a 2015 summer season are underway and will build on the success to date and the multilateral partnership that has steadily developed since 2008. Our work is far from complete. I am excited to anticipate the many stories *Erebus* will tell and what information she will reveal about the ultimate fate of the crew. And I am filled with renewed hope that our collective efforts will lead us to the final resting place of her sister ship, *Terror*.

As someone who was raised in the Arctic and heard first-hand our oral traditions, I feel this discovery has a very deep and personal importance to me. The Franklin expedition reveals so much about who we are as a nation and, in the spirit of such collaborative efforts, I am pleased to work with partners like The Royal Canadian Geographical Society so that Canadians, and people worldwide, can be inspired by this remarkable story. It is an honour and a pleasure to introduce The Royal Canadian Geographical Society's publication *Franklin's Lost Ship: The Historic Discovery of HMS* Erebus. I hope you enjoy reading this book as much as I have.

THE HONOURABLE LEONA AGLUKKAQ

FRANKLIN

INTRODUCTION

FOR ONE WHO HAS BEEN caricatured as the stolid embodiment of Britannic hubris, Captain Sir John Franklin is remarkable for his diverse characterizations. We know the essentials of the story of the 1845–1848 British Arctic expedition Franklin commanded—the deaths of all 129 officers and men, the bone scatter marking the path of their attempted retreat from the Arctic and, of course, the disappearance of the two exploration ships, HMS *Erebus* and HMS *Terror*. It was a mass disaster played out over several years, but it is often also one assigned to shortcomings in the character of Franklin himself, even though he was dead before the worst of it.

In her excellent introduction to my book *Frozen in Time: The Fate of the Franklin Expedition*, Margaret Atwood wrote about the different manifestations of Franklin over time, how he evolved with our culture, from the romantic Victorian hero of self- (and more generalized) sacrifice, whom Atwood calls Franklin Aloft, before coming down heavily to Earth as the Halfwit Franklin by the second half of the twentieth century, an allusion to the expedition's failure to adopt Inuit customs.

In recent years, Franklin's reputation has been on the move again, transformed into what might be called Franklin Disinterred, by the research led by my *Frozen in Time* co-author Owen Beattie, who applied forensic science to the Franklin mystery. In the process, the first physical evidence was found to support Inuit testimony of cannibalism among the last men standing, accounts carried to London by the overland explorer John Rae, setting off a round of knicker-tightening and racist slurs. The research also demonstrated that scurvy was a factor, as historians had long surmised, and produced the additional revelation that lead poisoning was afoot on the expedition, with the suspected chief culprit being the tinned food supply. Franklin's leadership abilities, or lack thereof, matter a whole lot less if he was, in Atwood's words, a victim "of bad packaging," with the result that lead had been coursing through his system.

Now, with the location of a ghostly, remarkably well-preserved hulk resting in frigid water in the general vicinity of where the Inuit had told nineteenth-century searchers that a ship had indeed sunk, we have yet another Franklin—Franklin Submerged.

This latest incarnation may prove to be the most fascinating and revelatory yet. The wreck found by the 2014 Victoria Strait Expedition was identified by Parks Canada's Underwater Archaeology Team as *Erebus*. It is Franklin's ship. Within the largely intact hull is Franklin's large cabin, the place where he lived, its built-in map drawers presumably filled with the charts he studied. Quite possibly his personal possessions are there, and who knows, maybe his bones too if the theories of some are correct. *Erebus* is, after all, where Franklin likely died.

On September 9, 2014, Prime Minister Stephen Harper, with Environment Minister Leona Aglukkaq seated on one side of him and Parks Canada's Ryan Harris on the other, announced to the country and the world the discovery of what was later confirmed to be *Erebus*, and by doing so he honoured both expeditions, Franklin's and the 2014 Victoria Strait Expedition, which, he said, had "solved one of Canada's greatest mysteries." He hailed the find as "truly a historic moment for Canada." This book is devoted to the significance of locating *Erebus*, but it is also intended to celebrate those partners that made it possible, led by Parks Canada and its Underwater Archaeology Team, an elite group of scientists who are also skilled divers. The team is led by Marc-André Bernier, and the lead for the Franklin search is Ryan Harris.

The expedition partnership was a formidable assertion of Canadian capability in the Arctic, embodied by people like the Royal Canadian Navy's Rear Admiral John Newton; senior archaeologist Douglas Stenton, director of heritage for the Government of Nunavut; Captain Bill Noon of the Canadian Coast Guard; Scott Youngblut of the Canadian Hydrographic Service; and Tom Zagon of the Canadian Ice Service.

Its unofficial CEO, if you will, was Jim Balsillie, the tech innovator, entrepreneur and co-founder of Research In Motion (BlackBerry), who helped invent the worldwide smartphone market. Balsillie is passionate about asserting Canada's place in the world, and that global view of a Canada punching above its weight extends to the Arctic, a realm where Canadian leadership is not only desirable but mandated by geography. Balsillie, together with Tim MacDonald, an equally passionate Canadian businessman, established the Arctic Research Foundation to assist in the Franklin search and to undertake other researches.

Its unofficial COO was Andrew Campbell, a vice president with Parks Canada at the time, and a mixture of public servant, diplomat, politician, holy man and best friend. He was a key to the partnership.

The Royal Canadian Geographical Society, an inheritor of the grand exploration traditions of Britain's Royal Geographical Society, was also a partner. The society is one of Canada's largest educational non-profits and the publisher of *Canadian Geographic*, the country's third-best-read magazine.

The society involved other non-government partners, all leaders in northern exploration. The W. Garfield Weston Foundation has invested hugely in support of northern science, among other initiatives establishing the prestigious Weston Family Prize for Lifetime Achievement in Northern Research. One Ocean Expeditions is world renowned for its polar expeditionary travel, and its managing director, Andrew Prossin, is a veteran expedition leader at either pole. Shell Canada has its own vast and far-reaching experience in Arctic resource exploration.

Of course, the fate of Franklin, and more particularly his ships, is not only one of Canada's great mysteries. It has also been a global exploration mystery for nearly seventeen decades, and nowhere more obviously than at home in the United Kingdom, where families mourned their losses, and where the confounding loss was keenly felt for decades, before Franklin's sacrifice was superseded by other, more modern polar tragedies.

Grandiose claims have been made for the significance of the find of *Erebus*. It has been likened in archaeological terms to the 1922 opening of Tutankhamun's tomb by Howard Carter and Lord Carnarvon. Certainly, in the context of exploration history, it is hard to imagine a more important discovery. There are plans underway to search for, as an example, Sir Ernest Shackleton's *Endurance*, a tremendously famous ship that was crushed and sank in the ice of the Weddell Sea in 1915, during his ill-starred Imperial Trans-Antarctic Expedition. But we know what happened to Shackleton. His experience was the polar opposite of Franklin's in that he and *Endurance*'s crew all lived. That is at the very foundation of Shackleton's legend. To find his ship would be a wonderful thing, but what might we learn? That's where *Erebus* differs from *Endurance*, and others, including the most famous of all shipwrecks, RMS *Titanic*. That is what makes this discovery so important, the possibility of what we might learn.

JOHN GEIGER

Parks Canada's *Investigator* dive boat was the platform for the first dives on the wreck of HMS *Erebus*.

CHAPTER 1

EXULTATION

EARLY SEPTEMBER 2014

QUEEN MAUD GULF, ARCTIC OCEAN

WHEN IT FINALLY HAPPENS, it happens fast. Inexorably, the sonar screen fills in, revealing the unmistakable shape of the ship, standing stoically at attention on the shallow seabed, as if it had been gently set there only days before.

In moments, the decades-long search comes to an end. Sir John Franklin's long-lost flagship, HMS *Erebus*, which he sailed from England in 1845 with the unquestioned confidence of all Britain that he would claim the elusive Northwest Passage, is found. Ryan Harris and Jonathan Moore, underwater archaeologists with Parks Canada, an agency of the Canadian government responsible not only for operating world-renowned parks such as Banff National Park but also for the preservation of national historic sites, are watching the screen. They have been doggedly hunting Franklin's lost ships for six seasons, peering at this screen year after year as sonar waves painstakingly trace the softly undulating seabed of the Arctic Ocean. Right now, as the ship's contours fill in, millimetre by millimetre, they can hardly believe their eyes.

For nearly seventeen decades, men have lost their good health and even their lives on this quest. Fortunes have been spent during these many generations of barren searching. Obsessions have swelled; imaginations have taken flight; myths have been born. But none of it has brought back Franklin's *Erebus* until this moment.

The sonar room of Parks Canada's survey boat *Investigator* is silent for one moment more. Then Harris cries out in sharp exultation. He and Moore each raise their hands high in the air and they slap them together in victory. The two men and technicians Chriss Ludin and Joe Boucher all embrace, jubilant, in triumph.

Theirs are the first non-Inuit eyes to see *Erebus* in just over 169 years.

EREBUS AND THE MEN who caught a glimpse of her on the floor of the Arctic Ocean were a few kilometres off the remote northern coast of North America among the scattershot islands that make up Canada's Arctic Archipelago at the frozen top of the world.

To protect the wreck from looters, the exact spot remains a closely guarded secret—as is the precise date the ship was discovered—but it is somewhere in the eastern Queen Maud Gulf about eighty kilometres south of the west flank of King William Island, an exceptionally bleak piece of land hundreds of kilometres above the treeline. Franklin, who reached the top tip of King William Island in 1846 with his two ships and most of the 133 men he set off with, likely thought the island was an extension of the North American mainland, as depicted on the charts of the day. So he directed his ships down the channel on this western side of the island through Victoria Strait, believing it was his only option to complete the passage.

It was a fatal calculation. Then, Victoria Strait was nearly unique in the southernmost waters of the Arctic Ocean for its propensity to freeze with ice so remorseless that it rebuffed the invitation to melt even in

Canada claims the Northwest Passage as territorial waters, and the waterway is patrolled by the country's Coast Guard, whose fleet of six icebreakers is the second largest in the world, after Russia's. The Coast Guard's duties there include search and rescue, and the escort of ships through icy waters, as the CCGS *Pierre Radisson* is seen doing here.

HMCS *Kingston* in the Davis Strait during the Victoria Strait Expedition.

The waters of Queen Maud Gulf are often placid, but high winds can be treacherous for ships large and small. Low-lying islands mean there is little to block the wind, and even the 90.5-metre *Sir Wilfrid Laurier* icebreaker was forced to spend several days at anchor when high winds blew into the gulf in September 2014.

The Franklin expedition's first winter was spent in the total darkness of the High Arctic, near Devon Island (pictured here), at 74 degrees north. Wintering in 1845–46 at a latitude even farther north than most Inuit settlements, the expedition experienced the loss of three crew members.

Space is at a premium on the MV *Martin Bergmann*. During the Victoria Strait Expedition, the ship housed archaeologists, journalists, navy personnel and the ship's crew. Bunks in the ship's bow sleep eight.

One Ocean Voyager navigates icy waters on its way to join the MV *Martin Bergmann* and CCGS *Sir Wilfrid Laurier* in Queen Maud Gulf.

the summer heat, making it impossible to sail potentially for years on end. *Erebus* and the second ship under Franklin's command, HMS *Terror*, warships fitted out specially to withstand the pressure of crushing ice, became imprisoned in the strait and were able to move only in tandem with the ice as it drifted, carrying them along. In a tragic irony, explorers who later came in search of Franklin discovered that King William is, in fact, an island and that the channel around its eastern side frees up reliably in the summer.

The Canadian Coast Guard icebreaker *Sir Wilfrid Laurier* played a central role in the Victoria Strait Expedition.

During the Victoria Strait Expedition, the CCGS *Sir Wilfrid Laurier* served as home base not only for members of the Coast Guard, but for searchers from Parks Canada and the government of Nunavut. From the ship's bridge, Captain Bill Noon surveys and manages operational excursions from the ship that range from search and rescue operations to archaeological surveying and scientific study.

HMCS *Kingston* at Pond Inlet.

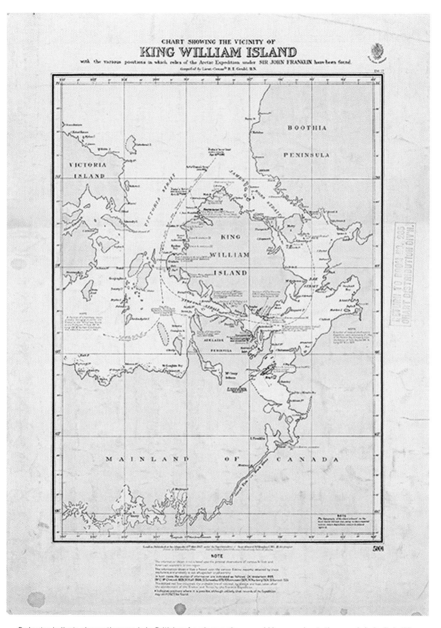

Red notes indicate observations made by British or American explorers, and blue ones denote those made by Inuit, in this 1927 map. Ultimately, the blue note indicating the presence of a ship in the vicinity of Wilmot and Crampton Bay proved correct. It was in this general area that *Erebus* was found in September 2014.

"Chart showing the vicinity of King William Island, with the various positions in which relics of the Arctic expedition under Sir John Franklin have been found," compiled by Lt-Commander R.T. Gould, Royal Navy, Admiralty Chart No. 5101, 1927. Library and Archives Canada

The communications equipment on the mast of MV *Martin Bergmann* was critical to the search for *Erebus*. Daily ice reports were retrieved via satellite Internet connection, GPS equipment relayed the ship's position relative to known hazards, and radio communications helped keep the crew safe, calling in the Coast Guard when the ship grounded on the then unknown Chidley Shoals.

With the CCGS *Sir Wilfrid Laurier* calling Victoria home and the Underwater Archaeology Team working from Ottawa, getting Parks Canada's gear on board the *Laurier* was no simple task. Some of their equipment and the *Investigator* survey and dive boat were driven to Nova Scotia before being carried north on the *One Ocean Voyager* and transferred to the *Laurier* in Arctic waters. Had the transfer not been successful, *Erebus* might have evaded discovery for another year.

Though July is the warmest month in the central Arctic, the window for Parks Canada's searchers doesn't begin until August. Only then, after months of near constant sunshine, has the ice of Queen Maud Gulf melted enough for side-scan sonar to be deployed. In a good year, the gulf will remain clear until late September, when the ice begins to set in for the long winter.

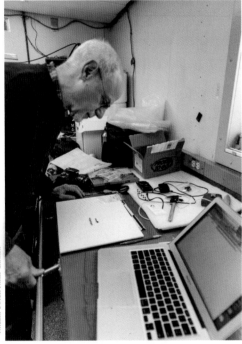

Nunavut's archaeological laws are strict and were developed in part by Nunavut's director of heritage Douglas Stenton, seen here in a lab on board the CCGS *Sir Wilfrid Laurier*. His terrestrial archaeological work led directly to the find of the *Erebus*.

Franklin and twenty-three others perished in the first three years of the expedition, already an unprecedented loss in the Victorian era's search for the Northwest Passage. Then in 1848, the savagely unlucky 105 survivors, fearing their vessels would never be set free, weakened by starvation, illness and lead poisoning, abandoned their ships and took to this polar desert island in search of salvation. Curiously, they did not follow the example of explorer John Ross, whose ship had been trapped the decade before in the ice off the Boothia Peninsula, the jut of land next to King William Island. Despite suffering from scurvy and near starvation, Ross's men trudged north to the whaling route of Lancaster Sound and were famously rescued. Nineteen of Ross's twenty-two men survived.

Franklin's men headed south instead to face the barrens of what is now northern Canada. It was a mass disaster in slow motion, spread out over many months. Total loss. No Franklin, no logbooks, no ships and no survivors. Some of the sailors' bones have been discovered, strewn haphazardly along the island's western and southern shores. Some of the skeletons show clear signs of having been butchered for food.

Despite dozens of searches beginning in 1848, no trace of Franklin himself has ever been found, apart from silverware utensils custom-made for him to take on the expedition and a few portable relics, such as his gold watch. The initial quest to find him was the most expensive rescue mission ever launched. At first, British searchers thought they might be able to find the men alive and bring them back home. Franklin's wife, Lady Jane Franklin, was a powerful force in galvanizing the effort and encouraging the British government. Eventually, however, the government abandoned hope of rescue and sought instead the recovery of his body and his ships. They did not succeed.

The tale of Franklin's unfathomable disappearance and the horrendous suffering of his men gripped the Victorian society he left behind and has continued to haunt

During the CCGS *Sir Wilfrid Laurier*'s Arctic missions, the Canadian Hydrographic Service works to improve Arctic charts. Here, hydrographer-in-charge Scott Youngblut installs equipment to ensure precise geographic coordinates.

Nunavut has thousands of archaeological sites, ranging from Inuit-built tent rings, cairns and inuksuit to artifacts left behind by European explorers like Sir John Franklin. Nunavut's weather and size are challenges for archaeologists like Douglas Stenton, shown here. Most fieldwork needs to be conducted when the land is snow-free, but even then sea ice frequently prevents access.

With a GPS beacon needing to be installed but its exact location unimportant, hydrographer Scott Youngblut (left) invited archaeologist Doug Stenton (centre) to choose an island of archaeological interest. Mentioning an intriguing tent ring, Stenton chose one. Once there, helicopter pilot Andrew Stirling (right) lent Stenton a hand and scoured the beach for artifacts, spotting the iron fitting that led to *Erebus*'s discovery.

Detail of the two broad arrows on the pintle found by Andrew Stirling and now part of the Government of Nunavut Collection.

No trees grow in the Queen Maud Gulf region, but it's not unusual to find wood on shore. Driftwood discharged by north-flowing rivers can float into the area, and Inuit hunting parties often leave behind wood from pallets or broken sled runners. So even though wood seems alien to the environment, helicopter pilot Andrew Stirling needed a keen eye to know the significance of the *Erebus* scuttle he'd found. The scuttle is now part of the Government of Nunavut Collection.

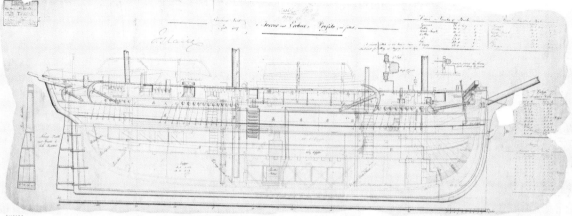

The extensive naval collection of the United Kingdom's National Maritime Museum includes plans for *Erebus* and *Terror*. Even though they are highly detailed, they leave important questions unanswered. Until now, archaeologists have speculated about puzzles such as the source of the locomotives used to power the ships' screw propellers, but dives on the wreck and potential excavation work will help reveal firmer answers to these mysteries.

The Canadian Hydrographic Service produces numerous charts of Canada's Arctic—like this one being used by Ryan Harris on board HMCS *Kingston* to illustrate the search area—but the region remains overwhelmingly uncharted. Charts lack critical data such as water depth and the location of shoals. The challenges faced by the hydrographic service are not unlike those Parks Canada encounters: the ice-free season is brief and northern logistics are complex.

Icy waters with CCGS *Sir Wilfrid Laurier* in the distance.

the imaginations of people all over the world. What went so catastrophically wrong with this expedition? How could such a finely outfitted and provisioned expedition, led by veterans of polar exploration, possibly have failed, and failed so grotesquely? It was as if Franklin's secrets were forfeit to the ocean depths along with the ship he commanded.

✦

TO SOME, THE REMARKABLE find of *Erebus* was not supposed to have happened the way it did. To others, veterans of the search, it was a foreseeable eventuality.

Harris, a carefully spoken yet witty man, and Moore, a bundle of exuberant energy with a wide smile at the ready, weren't meant to still be scanning for one of Franklin's wrecks in Queen Maud Gulf at that time, according to the project's schedule.

In fact, the Parks Canada team—along with new partners, brand-new, high-tech equipment and the continued personal blessing of Canada's prime minister, Stephen Harper—had plans to spend that part of the search season in Victoria Strait, where the other of Franklin's two ships is thought to have sunk. After several

The Underwater Archaeology Team needs to have a high degree of technical proficiency to operate in the Arctic. If a problem occurs with their gear, technicians are thousands of kilometres away, in places like Victoria or St. John's.

seasons of underwater investigation, large tracts of the seafloor there still needed to be searched.

The 2014 search for Franklin's missing ships was the most ambitious, most extensive, best-equipped and most elaborately planned that had been conducted, with the co-operation of an unprecedented number of public and private organizations. The Canadian government's participation alone represented an extraordinary partnership encompassing Parks Canada, the Royal Canadian Navy, the Canadian Coast Guard, the Canadian Ice Service, the Canadian Space Agency, the Canadian Hydrographic Service, and Defence Research and Development Canada. Sophisticated technology developed and built in three provinces—Nova Scotia, Newfoundland and British Columbia—was in play. The Government of Nunavut, the sprawling northernmost Canadian territory that encompasses most of Canada's Arctic Archipelago, including the islands in Queen Maud Gulf, was as always intricately involved in the plans.

A single private partner had been involved since 2010: the Arctic Research Foundation, co-founded by philanthropists Jim Balsillie and Tim MacDonald, which arranged to buy and outfit a boat, the MV *Martin Bergmann*, to be dedicated to the search. But by 2014, the private participation had grown to include The Royal Canadian Geographical Society, which brought along with it The W. Garfield Weston Foundation, One Ocean Expeditions and Shell Canada.

The result was the largest Franklin search since the early 1850s: an armada of four ships, including a Canadian Coast Guard icebreaker, two self-propelled underwater robots, several smaller vessels, sonar equipment and a crack team of divers. They were christened the 2014 Victoria Strait Expedition.

Bill Noon, captain of the Canadian Coast Guard icebreaker *Sir Wilfrid Laurier*, reflected at the start of the Victoria Strait Expedition in his online Captain's Log, dated August 30, 2014: "Our well deck is now at full capacity, with the two seven-metre CHS launches *Gannet* and *Kinglett* and the Parks Canada 10-metre *Investigator* tightly arranged around our hatch. And I shouldn't forget to mention the toys stored in the hold, including both the autonomous underwater vehicle and the remotely operated vehicle that Parks Canada brought up, in addition to our own ROV. The planning phase is now officially over, and our limitations now relate only to the number of crew available to operate the assets, the weather, and as always, the ice. . . . I think I have Franklin fever."

But Victoria Strait didn't co-operate. For the first time since 2009, the strait locked up with ice, meaning that the full team couldn't spend as much time there as planned. Instead, the strait's ice forced some of the

Cambridge Bay's relatively accessible location on the Northwest Passage has made it a centre for investment in the Arctic. The port served as a staging area for the searchers of the Victoria Strait Expedition, with the Coast Guard using its airport to resupply and transfer personnel, and the Arctic Research Foundation centring its northern operations in the community. It is also the location for the government's new Canadian High Arctic Research Station.

VALERIE WYNJA/ENVIRONMENT CANADA

vessels to stay in the ice-free Queen Maud Gulf, farther south. The gulf had been earmarked for the first phase of the summer search, but the plan had always been for all the vessels to push north and concentrate on the strait once the ice cleared.

At first, it seemed like bad luck. But serendipity began a few days before *Erebus* miraculously showed up on that screen—on a fateful Monday, September 1, 2014.

Douglas Stenton was in a helicopter looking to land on a small island in the eastern Queen Maud Gulf. Stenton, an archaeologist, is director of heritage for Government of Nunavut. Nunavut is the newest Canadian territory, created late in the twentieth century as part of a land claims settlement with the Inuit, whose nomadic ancestors began living off these lands and this ice thousands of years ago.

Stenton has devoted his career to Arctic archaeology and has spent years assessing accounts from the Inuit about their encounters with Franklin's desperate men and their foundering ships. One of the most revered modern Inuit historians is Louie Kamookak, who lives in Gjoa Haven, a hamlet of about 1,300 people and King William Island's only permanent human settlement.

Like so many involved in this search, Kamookak is consumed with the mystery of Franklin and the gruesome drama that played out all those years ago on the island he calls home. For years, he has collected books on Franklin's expeditions and the rescue literature that Franklin's disappearance spawned and cross-referenced them with the elders' stories. He has trekked to many of the sites that may hold clues to the Franklin mystery. In recent years, he has helped Stenton and the Parks Canada team to identify shorelines and islands that the Inuit tradition suggests are worth investigating.

On September 1, Stenton had no idea he was on the brink of discovering a new clue to the mystery. He was working with his colleague Scott Youngblut from the Canadian Hydrographic Service. Youngblut needed to find a location for a temporary Global Positioning System (GPS) station that would read messages from satellites in space and help map the depth of the ocean floor for general navigating. Stenton wanted to investigate a scatter of small islands for evidence of the lost ships. One island could serve both purposes; they set off. The choice Stenton proposed was within the southern search zone where Inuit accounts say one of Franklin's ships had sunk: Ookgoolik, the place of the bearded seals. But at that point, after years of searching by archaeologists and amateur explorers alike, particularly in the modern era from 1964, and then from 2008 onward by the Parks Canada–led team, no clear evidence of a Franklin wreck had been found.

From the air, Stenton pinpointed one of the tiny islands he was interested in and they set down. It had an ancient Inuit tent ring and it was the right distance away from the survey vessels to serve as a spot for the GPS station. Quickly, Stenton strode over to the tent ring, one of many in the Arctic, and began a routine archae-ological survey, taking photographs and measurements. Andrew Stirling, the Coast Guard helicopter pilot who had just landed their Messerschmitt-Bölkow-Blohm Bo 105, wandered along the shore. Stirling is not a professional archaeologist, just an enthusiastic, talented volunteer who had been thoroughly briefed on what to look for and what to do if something was found. Harris calls him a "fantastic artifact hound."

It was by chance that Stirling was there at all. He frequently drops off his passengers and then immediately departs for other aerial errands. But that day, he started scanning the water's edge, searching for anything that stood out from the rock-studded sand. And then, there it was. Something that didn't fit. A long piece of aged, rusted iron half-buried in the sand.

He knelt. What he saw was a sturdy, elongated U, similar to a tuning fork but heavy, nearly the length and breadth of a big man's arm. He called Stenton over. Stenton was flabbergasted. Both the size and shape of the iron piece were different from anything else he had seen to date. He got down on his hands and knees and examined it for a sign stamped into the metal that marked it as the property of the British government: the broad arrow, or crow's foot as it's sometimes known, essentially three converging lines in the shape of an upside down *V*. The stamp indicates that the British Crown's money has paid for the item, and it can be found on nearly every piece of material, right down to the nails, that made up ships of the royal fleet, a practice begun during the time of Henry VIII and now replaced by bar codes and stock numbers. Nothing.

At Stenton's request, Stirling picked up the iron piece out of the sand. It was photographed before Stir-ling handed it to Stenton, who peered at it intently, still looking for the stamped arrow, still hoping it might be a piece of one of Franklin's ships. He saw nothing. But then he saw two broad arrows. This heavy piece of iron had come from a Royal Navy ship.

Side-scan sonar operates via a sonar unit towed by a long steel cable, and the system is vulnerable to even moderate winds. Waves bounce the sonar unit around in the water, blurring the image that Parks Canada searchers like Jonathan Moore, pictured here (right) on the *Martin Bergmann*. When winds are favourable and waters are calm, searchers trade seats at the sonar screen around the clock to make the most of the window of opportunity.

Stenton knew there was a strong chance the piece had come from one of Franklin's ships.

The focus now turned to the beach. Again, Stirling found the prize: a weathered wooden artifact with an iron nail. It was likely a piece of a wrecked ship and possibly Franklin's own *Erebus*, the one he lived on and very likely died on. *Erebus*, the ship that may still contain his possessions and his journals, that may even contain his corpse and, along with all that, some of the answers to the enigma of his failure.

The men on the beach were stunned. Throughout the century and a half of searching, many artifacts from Franklin's expedition have surfaced. And they've been cherished, viewed almost as sacred relics as the legend of his mysterious failure grew. But most have been relatively small things, items carried off the ships, not debris from the lost warships. Many are now lodged at the National Maritime Museum in Greenwich, England. Earlier investigators of Franklin's fate brought them back, many bartered from Inuit who had taken them from the ships, from the detritus abandoned as the sailors left their ships and began a doomed journey toward an imagined rescue hundreds of kilometres distant.

In the original searches, an intact ship's boat containing "portions of two human [skeletons]" was discovered. But mainly, it had been bits of personal belongings that sailors would have brought from their homes in Britain in a quixotic urge to carry the conveniences of Victorian England with them to the wild wastes of the North. They are haunting reminders of the fragility and humanity of Franklin's men: fragments of a clay pipe; some shattered teacups; a pair of spectacles; a crumpled bootlace; the leather heel of a shoe, perfect for the British heaths, but desperately ill-suited to marching over slippery ice. The disintegrating remnants of a knitted woollen glove, heartbreakingly jaunty red stripes still visible, are particularly resonant. It's impossible not to imagine the hands that knitted that glove, the hands of the condemned man who wore them in a futile bid to keep out the cold.

But nothing of this scale. Nothing remotely suggesting the wreckage of the warships themselves. It was a clue. What if there were more, hidden below the water, tantalizingly close?

✦

That evening, Stenton and his colleague Robert Park, an archaeologist in the department of anthropology at the University of Waterloo in Ontario, were back on board the Coast Guard's icebreaker, CCGS *Sir Wilfrid Laurier*, named after Canada's first francophone prime minster, a man who was in office as Queen Victoria's reign was coming to an end and for a decade afterwards. The ship was their base for this year's expedition, and at that moment, they were closed in a laboratory with Harris, Moore, Youngblut, Bill Noon, *Laurier*'s captain, Rich Marriott, *Laurier*'s chief officer, and Theresa Nicholls, a Fisheries and Oceans communications officer. Land archaeologists conferring with underwater archaeologists (a standard operating procedure), consulting a long-time seafarer, all trying to figure out what the rusted piece of metal meant. (The distinctive wooden item was quickly identified as the scuttle for a large anchor chain, in other words, a cover for the deck hole through which a ship's chain would pass down into its stowage locker. This was a tantalizing find, as both *Erebus* and *Terror* were equipped with iron anchor chains.)

Noon, a lanky giant of a man who has long been fascinated by the search for Franklin, knew the second he saw the U-shaped metal piece that maritime history was being rewritten on his ship. They had never seen an artifact like this one. In all their years of searching and in all the years that went before, there had never been anything that held more promise that, finally, one of Franklin's ships might be close at hand. However, they puzzled over which part of a ship this piece of iron was.

To Noon, the iron piece the team found on the island in Queen Maud Gulf looked as though it might be part of the ship's rigging.

But the captain was frustrated. He's fond of saying that the sea has been in his blood from boyhood. He's a keen maritime historian and freely admits to having Franklin fever, the irrepressible urge to find out what happened on the doomed expedition. But, despite all his knowledge and passion, he couldn't figure out where the metal would have fit into Franklin's ship.

Finally, Moore turned to his computer and pulled up detailed blueprints of *Erebus* and *Terror*. He pored over them, comparing the shape of this heavy piece of metal to what he knew was on each ship. Piece by piece.

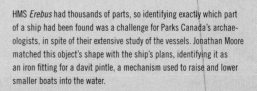

Midship Section

HMS *Erebus* had thousands of parts, so identifying exactly which part of a ship had been found was a challenge for Parks Canada's archaeologists, in spite of their extensive study of the vessels. Jonathan Moore matched this object's shape with the ship's plans, identifying it as an iron fitting for a davit pintle, a mechanism used to raise and lower smaller boats into the water.

JONATHAN MOORE/PARKS CANADA

Parts of Canada's Arctic were given British-sounding names by the dozens of search parties that sought out signs of Franklin's lost expedition. Surprisingly, the Royal Geographical Society Islands (seen here) at the bottom of Victoria Strait did not get their name that way. The islands were named by Norwegian Roald Amundsen, who completed the first successful transit of the Northwest Passage in 1906. The society was among Amundsen's sponsors.

NICK WALKER/*CANADIAN GEOGRAPHIC*

And then, not half an hour later, he found it. It was the lower piece of a davit, an apparatus fixed to the side of the ship and used to lift boats in and out of the water. This metal piece was called a pintle, a sort of cradle to hold the hefty timber arm upright as it lifted a boat. It was exactly the same as the ones on *Erebus* and *Terror*.

It made sense. If a ship had sunk in shallow water, the ice would have closed in over top, fixing her like a fly in amber. But then more ice would have moved in on top and ripped away the masts that were still sticking out above the surface of the sea. A snarl of rigging and the shrouds from the masts would have wrenched a davit up from the side of the ship. Then all of it would have been carried off, some to land. But because it was so heavy, it likely wouldn't have been carried far.

After that, there was no doubt. The next day, Harris and Moore would set out with technicians Ludin and Boucher in the Parks Canada boat *Investigator* and deploy their sonar gear just offshore from the island where the pintle and scuttle had been found. Now the quest for Franklin was feeling terribly focused.

FOR ALL THE YEARS that have passed since Franklin's voyage, for the gradually increasing presence of the Canadian government in the Arctic and all the sophisticated technology that has been developed in more than a century and a half, Queen Maud Gulf is still largely uncharted, like 90 per cent of Canada's Arctic waters. The most recent navigation charts date from the middle of the last century, and they're often wrong. Not only that, but the islands lie low in the water, barely above sea level, and their shape changes with the tides. Sailing here, searching in what are usually shallow waters, is incredibly tense. And dangerous.

When the Parks Canada team first looked here in 1997, then again starting in 2008 (following in the footsteps of other searchers in previous years), the contours of the shoreline and the location—even the existence—of islands was not always clear. In some cases, the maps that navigators were working with showed a shoreline as much as four kilometres away from where it should have been. Islets and islands turned out to be phantoms, and dangerous underwater seabed formations were not even marked.

During the Victoria Strait Expedition, even after several years of intensive searches in this part of the Arctic by the Parks Canada and Canadian Hydrographic Service crews, the hydrographers from the latter were making charts as they went along, referencing notes from earlier years, earlier expeditions, and then constantly revising them. It's such a remote part of the planet that when one of the ships engaged in the Parks Canada–led search for Franklin arrives here, it's sometimes the first ship ever to sail in these precise waters.

In six years of searching, the Parks Canada team saw only a single boat from the two nearest hamlets—Gjoa Haven and Cambridge Bay—although some of the hunters from those communities come over the ice in the winter in search of game.

Even the wildlife doesn't favour this unusually forlorn part of the Arctic expanse. The islands, with their low-lying limestone bases surrounded by shallow water, have a covering of sand. That sand supports few plants, and small ones at that, so animals go elsewhere for their food. A few islands are home to a handful of muskox, diminutive creatures with long, shaggy fur, curved horns and nourishing meat; but even they are sparse. And caribou, one of the food staples of the Inuit, are not plentiful.

Unlike so much of the Arctic, which has breathtaking mountains formed long ago by the gyrations of warring tectonic plates and vast, swift-flowing glacial rivers and lakes, the landscape on King William Island is sedate. Geologists joke that if they siphoned all the water off Queen Maud Gulf, they would end up with the prairies. The drama in this part of the world comes not from its geological past or its biological riches, but from its anguished human history and the efforts to find out what happened.

✦

It was tedious work, monitoring the sonar screen, looking for the underwater wreck of Franklin's ships. After six seasons, the Parks Canada team had it down to a fine art. They set the side-scan sonar unit—a silver cylinder called a towfish, just over a metre long—to the higher of its two frequencies so that its acoustic images would be crisp. (The lower frequency gives fuzzier images more apt to miss something.) Then they towed it behind their small Parks Canada boat, *Investigator*, with a cable. It swam over the sea floor, sending regular pulses of sound down to the bottom of the ocean, reaching out to one hundred metres on either side.

Ping—the sound waves hit the bottom of the ocean. *Ping*—they bounced back up to the towfish in a distinctive pattern—instantly relayed up the tow cable and translated into a computer image of the bottom and anything on it. It was like having a pair of eyes scanning the ocean floor in a swath two hundred metres wide.

They steered the boat along a precise grid of survey lines set 150 metres apart: up one line and then down the other. Over and over. Missing nothing. They likened it to mowing the lawn. The men on the team who were from Prince Edward Island called it planting potatoes, in honour of that province's prized crop. And while the sonar pinged, either Harris or Moore scrutinized the screen to see if it was picking anything up. Mostly, it didn't. Mostly, it was screen after screen of sand and gravel, staggeringly, monotonously the same.

But that day, they were searching right off the island where Stirling and the archaeologists had found the pintle and the piece of wood, and there was no monotony at all. For the first time in all these years, they knew they could possibly be right on top of one of Franklin's ships. And conditions were in their favour: the day was sunny, the sky was clear. There was hardly any wind and the ocean was as calm as glass.

Harris was at the end of his very first line of the grid and handing the watch over to Moore when things went wrong. The towfish, swimming behind the boat, nearly hit one of those uncharted shoals. Moore was frantic. The last thing he wanted was for the technology to be damaged just as the team could be on the cusp of a big discovery. He reeled in the towfish while Boucher at the helm hit the throttle, both trying to get the device higher up the water column so it wouldn't crash.

Moore was focused on saving the towfish. Harris was looking over his shoulder, ready to leap in. Harris glanced at the screen. Suddenly, it wasn't the monochrome of sand and gravel anymore. Suddenly, the shape of a ship formed unmistakably on the screen.

It was *Erebus*.

Among the first side-scan sonar images of HMS *Erebus* at its discovery, this page and next.

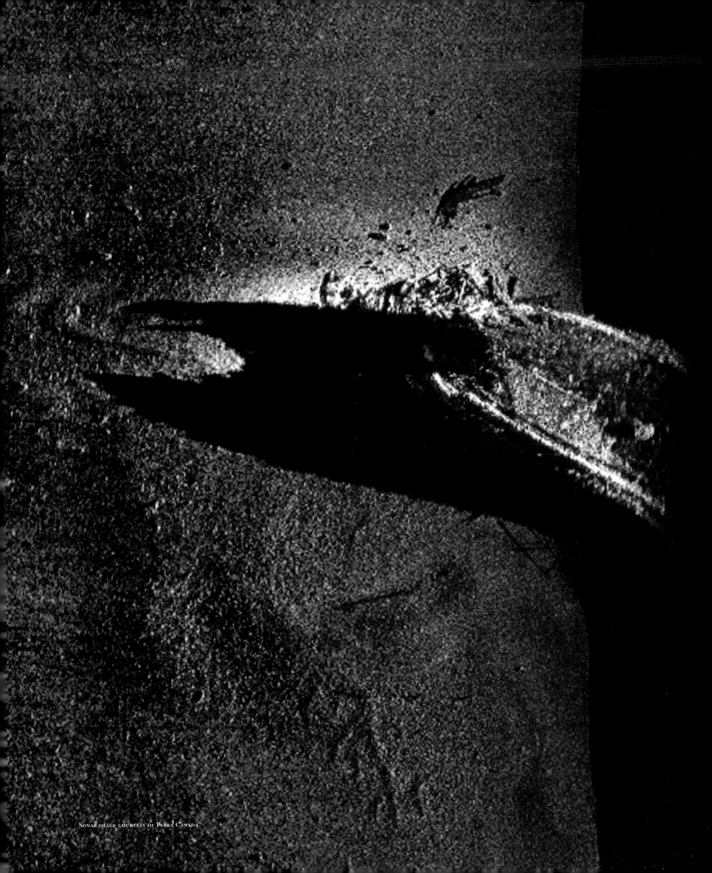

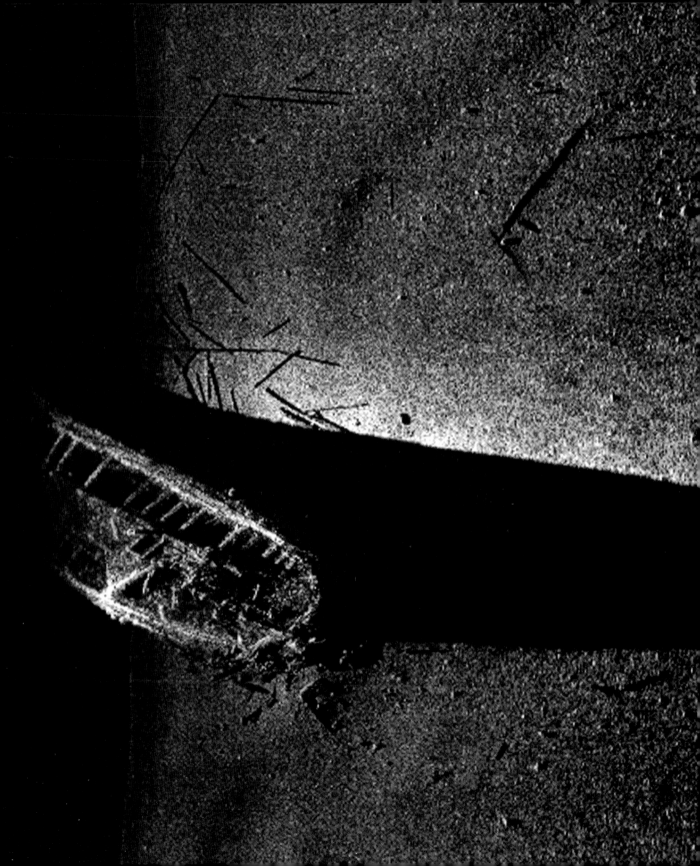

HMS *Erebus* and HMS *Terror*, shown in *The Illustrated London News*, May 24, 1845.

CHAPTER 2

TRIUMPHAL DEPARTURE

May 19, 1845

London

THE TWO SHIPS, *Erebus* and *Terror*, were heavily laden, towed by steam-powered propeller sloop down the River Thames to the ocean. Each was freshly painted an imposing jet-black, cut with a wide yellow stripe running from stem to stern above the waterline. The banks were thronged with Londoners who had come out to watch them depart, cheering the assured success of Sir John Franklin, the fabled Arctic explorer, as he sailed away to lay claim to the Northwest Passage for Britain.

Men had been trying to find the route across the top of North America—the watery link between Europe and the Orient—since Henry VII was on the throne. All had failed. But that time, early in the reign of Queen Victoria, the voyage seemed destined for success.

Those were confident times. The British, recent vanquishers of Napoleon, were the acknowledged global masters of sea and land. The British Empire was the world's unrivalled economic and industrial powerhouse in the midst of the century of its strongest expansion. London, its cultural and financial centre, was the biggest, richest city in the world, two million strong.

And the conquering of the northern polar region was one of the few important geographical discoveries left on the roster in the great nineteenth-century age of exploration. To John Barrow, second secretary to the Admiralty and the most fervent driver of polar exploration, finding the Northwest Passage was a geographical prize that was Britain's by right. Even some of the 133 men who sailed with Franklin in 1845 believed that they would reach the Pacific Ocean by the following summer, unscathed and victorious, national heroes. They would be lauded for having made scientific advances, and would collect the lavish ten-thousand-pound

In the golden age of exploration, British explorers were celebrities seen as bringing glory to an empire at its apex. Sir John Franklin was immortalized on trading cards—which then came in cigarette packages—and in heroic and idealized images like this one, made thirty years after his death.

reward Britain offered to those who finally penetrated the passage's mysteries, more than a million dollars in today's money.

More than just the geopolitical and national omens were favourable. As the convoy was bidding England farewell, a dove settled on the mast of *Erebus*, Franklin's own ship, and remained there. To some of the well-wishers, this was a prophecy that triumph was at last at hand. They saw it as a clear nod to the biblical story of Noah, who, marooned on his boat during the flood, searching desperately for land, sent off a dove that returned with an olive leaf: the promised land was nearby.

FEW SHIPS IN THE HISTORY of ocean exploration have been as marked for triumph as *Erebus* and *Terror*. For one thing, they were opulently provisioned. Franklin, captain of *Erebus*, had on board his own set of newly made fiddle-patterned silverware stamped with his family crest—a conger eel between two branches—and a personal steward to serve him his meals and keep his possessions in order. A library of nearly three thousand books was laid in for leisurely reading on the two ships, including some of Shakespeare's works, Charles Dickens's *Nicholas Nickleby*, the Bible and other religious tomes, and Oliver Goldsmith's happy-ever-after romance *The Vicar of Wakefield*, a Victorian favourite. There was a hand organ on each vessel, mahogany writing desks and even a daguerreotype apparatus for taking photographs, a most modern innovation that Franklin's voyage was the first expedition to enjoy. The upper-class trappings of Victorian England were sailing in full complement to the barren Arctic.

There was plenty of food to feed all 134 men for as many as three years. Much of the food was preserved by recent technology: tin cans whose seams were soldered with lead. This innovation—so new that the can opener had not yet been invented—was hailed as a brave, longed-for advance in ocean exploration.

Between them, the two ships carried nearly eight thousand tins of preserved meats, adding up to about twenty-four tonnes, including boiled and roasted and seasoned beef, seasoned ox cheek, boiled and roasted mutton, veal, plus tinned root vegetables and soup and tinned pemmican. In addition, there were nearly thirty-five tonnes of flour, nearly two tonnes of tobacco, 7,560 litres of wine and rum, plus chocolate, many chests of tea and the necessary lemon juice, a bid to prevent the scourge of scurvy among men who might not eat fresh food for years on end.

The ships themselves had been transformed from naval bomb barques, designed to lie close to shore during an attack and bombard the enemy from close range, into marvels of modern seafaring technology. They were built for polar survival, lumberers rather than sprinters. Each had had a small, second-hand coal-fired railway locomotive engine and smokestack installed, designed to run a propeller capable of moving the ship through open leads in the ice, yet with a very limited supply of coal. But they were not icebreakers. *Erebus*'s engine was twenty-five horsepower; *Terror*'s was twenty. Modern icebreakers are forty thousand. The engines were in addition to the traditional three masts and rigging and sails. The propellers, attached by shafts that ran a third of the length of the ship from the stern to the engine, could be moved to a holding area just inside the ship's frame when the winds were fair. That was so they wouldn't get damaged when not in use, or impede progress if the ships were sailing well under the wind. The ships, which had been refitted so their parts could be interchanged if one faltered, also featured a heating apparatus that would help warm the sleeping quarters on board, a concession to the Arctic cold.

Not only that, but the ships' oaken hulls were heavily reinforced for the journey with extra wood planking to help them withstand the thrusts of ice, and then iron plates layered on top of the wood stretching six metres on either side of the prow. Inside, each had extra bracing across its width,

HULTON ARCHIVE/GETTY IMAGES

Mid-19th-century expeditions needed ingenuity to light their ships. The semicircle at the top of this illustration of James Fitzjames's cabin on HMS *Erebus* is a type of prism known as an illuminator. These were installed on a ship's deck to allow light to shine below. The wood engravings pictured here first appeared in *The Illustrated London News*, May 24, 1845.

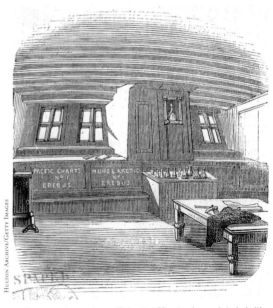

HULTON ARCHIVE/GETTY IMAGES

Space was at a premium on *Erebus*. Just 32 metres long and stocked with provisions to last 134 men three full years, living space was limited. It was not the captain who bore the brunt of these spatial limitations. Sir John Franklin's quarters were modest by the standards of Victorian officers but roomy viewed through the lens of Arctic exploration.

Franklin knew the Arctic winter was long, dark and dull. Keeping the crew occupied was a priority. Hunting and scouting missions would have prevented idleness, and the ships had an extensive library. They also carried more than 7,500 litres of rum and wine. That sounds like a lot, but split between 134 men over three years, it is just over 300 millilitres per week, only slightly more than a standard glass of red wine.

constructed with beams twenty-five centimetres thick. *Erebus*, the slightly larger of the two and the more important, because it carried Franklin himself, was also reinforced with iron braces fitted diagonally across the inside of its hull. The decks of both ships were made with the traditional planks set lengthwise in addition to a second layer of planks set on the diagonal, the better to absorb shocks and pressure from the grinding ice. Each had two Massey patent double-action (lift and force) brass bilge pumps, the latest technology, to rid the wooden ships of the water they were bound to take on during the voyage. These were no ordinary vessels.

And, of course, the ships were protected by their fearsome names and reputations. Erebus, in both Greek and Roman traditions, is a place of darkness between Earth and Hell, a sort of dusky limbo of endless horror. "Terror" is something that intimidates or causes dread. These ships had been navy workhorses for years. *Erebus*, nearly twenty years old, had done service in the Mediterranean and was famous for having helped to navigate through Antarctica's icy waters just four years earlier, along with *Terror*.

The Franklin expedition wasn't HMS *Terror*'s first journey into Canada's Arctic, nor the first time it fell prey to Arctic ice. Sir George Back led an expedition aboard *Terror* in 1836–37. The ship was iced in for 10 months near Southampton Island, suffering severe damage to its stern before managing to return across the Atlantic while taking on water.

Terror, more than thirty years old, was a grizzled veteran, much mended. The ship had a hallowed history of warfare. Her most renowned war engagement was the Battle of Baltimore, the second battle of the War of 1812 between British and American land and sea forces. She launched a volley of rockets—with their red glare—at Fort McHenry, which inspired the lyrics of the song that was to become the American anthem, "The Star-Spangled Banner." *Terror* had already done a tour of duty in Antarctica. And she had a history in the Arctic ice, too. Famously, she was badly damaged during a miserable voyage in the Arctic under the command of George Back in the 1830s—he wrote that the ship "creaked as if it were in agony"—forced at one point up onto shore on a fearsome angle by the frozen contortions of the ice.[1] She survived the ordeal; it added to her lore.

The medium of photography was emerging as the Franklin expedition set sail, giving us a realistic look at Sir John Franklin immediately before the journey. This daguerreotype image is crude, but revealing enough to show an aging captain about to take on the mission that would prove to be his match.

AS *EREBUS* AND *TERROR* made their way to Greenland, Franklin was feeling primed for victory. And he no doubt welcomed it. Franklin was looking to polish his reputation.

He had recently returned to England in disgrace, removed from his position as lieutenant-governor of Van Diemen's Land, an island state now known as Tasmania, part of the Australian commonwealth. A reformer, he had fallen afoul of his colonial secretary, John Montagu, who accused him of being unduly influenced by his wife, Lady Jane Franklin. Montagu, who still had influential friends in London, engineered his ouster. Franklin would eventually be vindicated and remembered as an able administrator, but at that moment, he felt the humiliation all too keenly.

Discovering the Northwest Passage would be his redemption. At fifty-nine, some of his peers considered him too old to be leading this taxing expedition, with all the rigours of Arctic privation. But there he was, ensconced on his ship, surrounded by his men and the highest cultural objects the Victorian age had to offer, in charge of a quest to claim one of the Empire's biggest geographical prizes. He wrote to a Tasmanian friend: "No one ever embarked on an expedition with more causes of rejoicing than ourselves—it is not therefore to be wondered at that we commenced our hazard in the highest spirits and full of hope that it may please God to prosper our effort to successful termination."[2]

He was where he wanted to be. He had been at sea much of the time since the age of fourteen. And he had a formidable record. He had been shipwrecked and cast away for two weeks off the coast of Australia early in his career. He had fought in the most decisive naval engagement in the Napoleonic Wars, the fabled Battle of Trafalgar. He survived a deadly land voyage he led to explore the frozen expanses of northern North America, coming so close to starvation that he became known as the man who ate his boots. He then led a second, much more successful expedition across the barren lands. He was convinced that he could make a success of this new commission. The president of The Royal Geographical Society, Sir Roderick Murchison, spoke for many when he remarked that Franklin's name was "a national guarantee."[3]

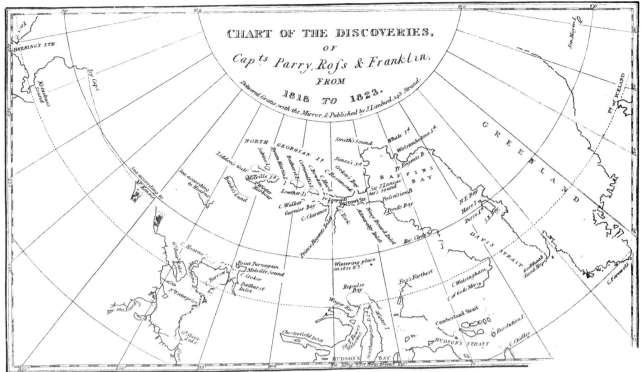

A chart of the discoveries of British Arctic explorers Sir William Edward Parry (1790–1855), Sir John Ross (1777–1856) and Sir John Franklin (1786–1847) in their attempts to find the Northwest Passage between Europe and Asia.

A small miracle had already occurred. Almost since he returned to England from Van Diemen's Land, Franklin had been ill with the flu. In a rare daguerreotype image taken before he set sail, he looked old and rheumy, especially compared to the youthful, robust men he would be commanding. But, for the first time since his return to Britain, he was feeling better. A cough he had had for months had vanished. In a letter he sent home by another ship before the expedition went incommunicado in the frozen Arctic, he told a niece:

> *You will be glad to know the coming to sea has had its usual good effect on me . . . I never in fact was in better health. I have every reason also to be happy—blessed as I am by having zealous & good young officers—and an active well disposed crew.*[4]

In May 1845, 134 officers and men had left Greenhithe, England, but when the ships headed into the Arctic after stopping at Disko Bay, Greenland, 129 were aboard. Five men had been sent back due to illness or other reasons. Many of the crew were drawn from the ranks of the navy, idled in the years since the defeat of Napoleon and eager to be back at sea.

In fact, life on *Erebus* and *Terror* was blithe and well organized. Franklin's second-in-command on *Erebus*, Commander James Fitzjames, was a wonderful chronicler of his shipmates' frame of mind and

LIEUT. COUCH, (MATE.)   LIEUT. FAIRHOLME.   C. H. OSMER, (PURSER.)   LIEUT. DES VŒUX. (MATE.)

CAPTAIN CROZIER. (" TERROR.")   CAPTAIN SIR JOHN FRANKLIN, K.H.C.   COMMANDER FITZJAMES. (CAPTAIN.—" EREBUS.")

Among those on *Erebus* and *Terror*, Franklin (this page, bottom row, centre) is best known. Yet other men played key roles. To Franklin's left, Francis Crozier was captain of HMS *Terror* and co-led the expedition once Franklin died. To the right of Franklin is James Fitzjames, whose written accounts tell us much of what we know of the expedition's early days. These sketches, which appeared in *The Illustrated London News* in 1851, are based on daguerreotypes from 1845.

LIEUT. GRAHAM GORE, (COMMANDER.)

S. STANLEY. (SURGEON.)

LIEUT. H. T. D. LE VESCONTE.

LIEUT. R. O. SARGENT. (MATE.)

JAMES READ. (ICE-MASTER.)

H. D. S. GOODSIR. (ASSISTANT-SURGEON.)

COLLINS. (2ND MASTER.)

PORTRAITS OF CAPTAIN SIR JOHN FRANKLIN, AND HIS CREW. —(SEE NEXT PAGE.)

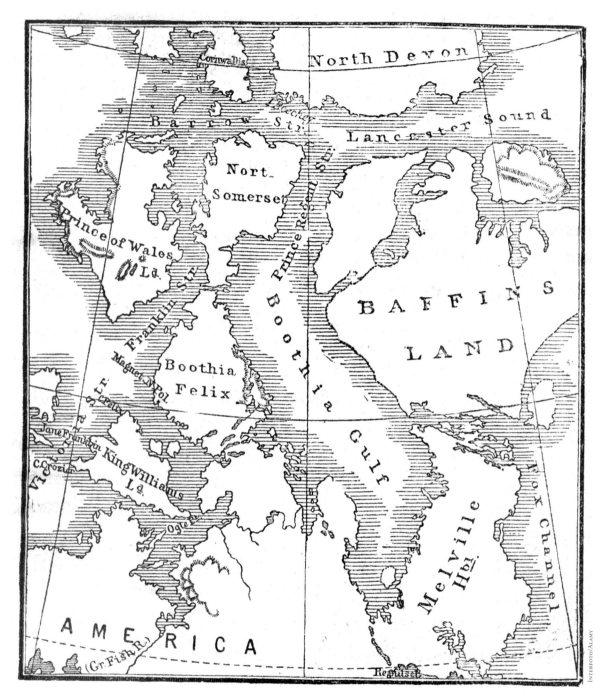

A single navigational choice could have changed the Franklin expedition's outcome. The now-established route of the Northwest Passage loops southeast of King William Island, through Simpson Strait, but Franklin chose the more direct route to the island's west via ice-prone Victoria Strait, believing the island was part of the mainland. Had he known of the narrow, windy strait to the island's south, the expedition might have accomplished its aims.

he sent the first of his journals back to England from Greenland. He painted the picture of men relaxed about the expedition, engaged in their discoveries, well-treated by their officers and confident in Franklin, their leader, who, as the Franklin scholar Leslie Neatby put it, was friendly, direct and devout, given to passionate preaching every Sunday.[5]

Fitzjames described[6] the mishaps of a handful of crew members during their last night in Britain—a stopover in Stromness in Scotland's Orkney Islands—who enthusiastically overindulged in drink, stole a boat in high spirits and rowed back to shore after they'd been booked in for the night. They were quickly rumbled and forced to return to the ship in the wee hours of the morning. One, an elderly sailor who had not been home for four years, was savouring a long farewell with his wife. In a rare act of naval clemency, they were not punished, but Fitzjames confiscated their liquor and had it thrown into the sea. The men were, in consequence, devoted to him.

Fitzjames drew an unforgettable image of Harry Goodsir, the Scottish surgeon and naturalist, who walked on the tips of his toes and was one day "in ecstasies" as he examined an unknown marine creature that resembled a "bag full of blubberlike stuff" under the "meecroscope." The gruff Scottish ice master, James Reid, who had cut his teeth reading the strategy of ice on Arctic whaling vessels, was horrified when *Erebus* installed a crow's nest, a

The excitement of Arctic exploration captured the imagination of Victorian Britain, but many illustrators had never ventured out of temperate climes. Their vision of the polar realm was a fantastical one.

A heroic Sir John Franklin, depicted here in the book *The Drawing Room of Eminent Personages*, published in 1860.

barrel fixed to the masthead, so that he could catch clearer glimpses of the obstacles ahead. It was too expensive, the frugal Scot declared; a frill.

One of the final images Fitzjames drew was of some of the men in the mess, drinking whisky and offering up toasts to the women in their lives. Since he had none, Fitzjames drank to his own future promotion, once the expedition returned home in glory.

⟡

THE NORTHWEST PASSAGE held a particular pull for the people of the nineteenth century. They longed to see themselves as the highest and best of God's creatures in a highly organized, symmetrical, idealized universe.[7] And since explorers had found a single route under the southern tip of South America, it stood to reason that, by the inflexible laws of symmetry, there must be a similar, single, obvious passage above the top of North America. Franklin was not looking for *a* route from Atlantic to Pacific; he was looking for *the* route. Because vast swaths of the Arctic Ocean were uncharted, there was little to contradict that idea.

The Arctic meant more to the citizens of the age than a new trade route or a geographical badge of honour. It had evolved into a rich, conflicted metaphor of romance and heroism—a symbol of the conquest of man over nature, seat of the Romantic ideal. It was the zone of the marvellous, the unexpected, the fantastical. Henry Hudson, writing of his explorations there more than two centuries earlier, remarked casually and with no further explanation that he came across a mermaid, and Luke Fox wrote in the same century that he spotted an ostrich.[8]

In fact, there was a highly textured polar genre at play, not only in the literature of Arctic exploration, which the people of the nineteenth century feasted on unabashedly, but also, as the Canadian novelist Margaret Atwood pointed out in her introduction to *Frozen in Time: The Fate of the Franklin Expedition*, in drawings that paint the Arctic as a "potent Otherworld . . . complete with otherworldly light effects, glittering ice-palaces, fabulous beasts—narwhals, polar bears, walruses—and gnome-like inhabitants dressed in exotic fur outfits."[9]

In some quarters, the Arctic was thought of as a polar paradise, a watery Eden, a place of eternal light and even warmth, a final empty frontier that the British could patch their culture onto wholesale. Many, including Barrow of the Admiralty and other proponents of Franklin's expedition, believed that the North Pole was in the centre of a warm, open sea, surrounded by an inconvenient icy barrier that developed navigable fissures in the spring. One had only to penetrate the barrier to sail freely across the Arctic Ocean and reach the Pacific. It was a lucrative new trade route just waiting to be plied.

That image was fed by such writings as the 1786 letter by Captain James Wyatt, published in *The Ipswich Journal*, which described reaching the high Arctic, only to find a warm open sea, mild weather and a "huge polar volcano sitting over the North Pole, spewing phosphorescent nitrous crystals."[10]

Mary Shelley, writing her novel *Frankenstein* in the early nineteenth century, captured the sentiment in the words of her character Robert Walton, the Arctic explorer:

> *I try in vain to be persuaded that the pole is the seat of frost and desolation; it ever presents itself to my imagination as the region of beauty and delight. There . . . the sun is for ever visible; its broad disk just skirting the horizon, and diffusing a perpetual splendour. There . . . snow and frost are banished; and, sailing over a calm sea, we may be wafted to a land surpassing in wonders and in beauty every region hitherto discovered on the habitable globe.*

As Atwood wrote, few Europeans had ever been to the Arctic. It was hard for them to imagine piercing cold persisting for months on end, a sun that failed to rise, ice that remained unyielding for years. But it was easy to imbue it with one's own romantic ideas, "a place where a hero might defy the odds, suffer outrageously, and pit his larger-than-usual soul against overwhelming forces."

Franklin was not fooled by the tales of a warm Arctic. He had already made two gruelling overland journeys to help map the northern shore of North America at the bottom of the Arctic Ocean, and had made one Arctic voyage by ship. He was familiar with the ice and cold but convinced that he and his men could conquer both. Like other Victorians, he believed that the multiple failures to find a navigable passage, dating from the late 1400s, only meant that more attempts were in order. It was the triumph of metaphor and theory over evidence. To doubt that the passage was discoverable was to doubt the power of man to control the elements, to confront the ice with his power, to know that he could bend it to his will. It was to doubt that the British ruled the waves, frozen or not. As Shelley's Walton concluded, "This ice cannot withstand you if you say that it shall not."

An illustration of *Erebus* and *Terror* as they sail into the ice floes of Baffin Bay.

To Franklin, the expedition was also his contribution to his generation's grand "magnetic crusade," a bid to understand, for the first time, how the Earth functioned as a giant magnet with a pole at either end—North and South—as the Franklin historian Andrew Lambert has documented. Called "geomagnetism," this was the burning scientific puzzle of the day—the biggest remaining mystery of the physical world, now that Newton had discovered gravity—and Franklin had already been keenly involved in it for years. During his tenure in Van Diemen's Land, he had helped set up an observatory to take measurements of magnetism.

Understanding geomagnetism was important in that era because travel by sea relied on the magnetic compass, which in turn depends on knowing where the magnetic pole is. Because the poles shift around and because the pull is inside the Earth, the closer one gets to a pole, the more the magnetic force dips below the surface of the planet, interfering with compass readings. Few magnetic compass measures of latitude and longitude in the Arctic (or, of course, the Antarctic), either on land or at sea, were accurate. In fact, they were erratic. Maddeningly, there was no system or formula to correct them. It was like a great magnetic hole at the top of the world. And when one's empire depended on trustworthy sea navigation, as Britain's did, this was a serious threat to power. Not only that, but the British knew that the force of their empire was not merely military or naval. It relied upon showing the world that they had mastered science and technology.

So scientists, particularly the British, were determined to crack the mysteries of magnetism. Driven by the Irish astronomer Sir Edward Sabine, they set up a network of observatories around the world to develop global models of the Earth's magnetic field. Sabine desperately wanted one in the Arctic, and Franklin was determined to put one there for him. It involved discovering not just the Northwest Passage but also tracking the magnetic North Pole. If Franklin succeeded, he would help scientists precisely calculate every seafaring route on the planet for the first time.

To that end, not only were *Erebus* and *Terror* carrying years' worth of food, not only were they ice-proofed to the best of the era's ability, but they were also carrying enough cutting-edge scientific equipment to set up at least one magnetic observatory in the Arctic. In fact, together they contained as much magnetic monitoring equipment as existed in any British colony in the world. Franklin and his officers had been trained in the latest methods of taking geomagnetic readings. The Arctic was not just a frontier of exploration; it was also a frontier of science. Franklin was at the centre of both, determined to triumph.

✦

THE EXPEDITION REACHED the western coast of Greenland, on the brink of entering the Northwest Passage, and the crew was in fine fettle. Ten oxen, which had been carried on a smaller vessel travelling alongside Franklin's ships, were slaughtered and stowed on board *Erebus* and *Terror*. The men sent letters and journals home, infused with happiness and with confidence about the adventures to come.

The final European glimpse of them came from the crews of two whaling ships. Franklin and his 128 men were waiting for a good wind to push them west from Greenland, across the expanse of Baffin Bay and into Lancaster Sound, the easternmost mouth of the Northwest Passage. All's well, the whaler's captain recorded in his log. Franklin's men were "in remarkable spirits, expecting to finish the operation in good time."[11]

It was July 28, 1845. No non-Inuit eyes would see *Erebus* for 169 years, one month and a handful of days, until Ryan Harris and Jonathan Moore, underwater archaeologists with the parks agency of Canada, a country that did not yet exist in 1845, saw its wreck on a screen in Queen Maud Gulf.

With fjords that present as channels, ever-changing ice conditions and hazardous straits, identifying a navigable route across Canada's North required learning from both earlier explorers and the Inuit's knowledge of the land. The Franklin expedition intended to use knowledge collected by earlier explorers like John Ross, shown here speaking with Inuit about the possibility of a Northwest Passage. This illustration first appeared in John Ross's *A Voyage of Discovery, Made under Orders of the Admiralty in His Majesty's Ships* Isabella *and* Alexander, *for the Purpose of Exploring Baffin's Bay, and Inquiring into the Probability of a North-West Passage* (London: J. Murray, 1819).

DE AGOSTINI PICTURE LIBRARY/GETTY IMAGES

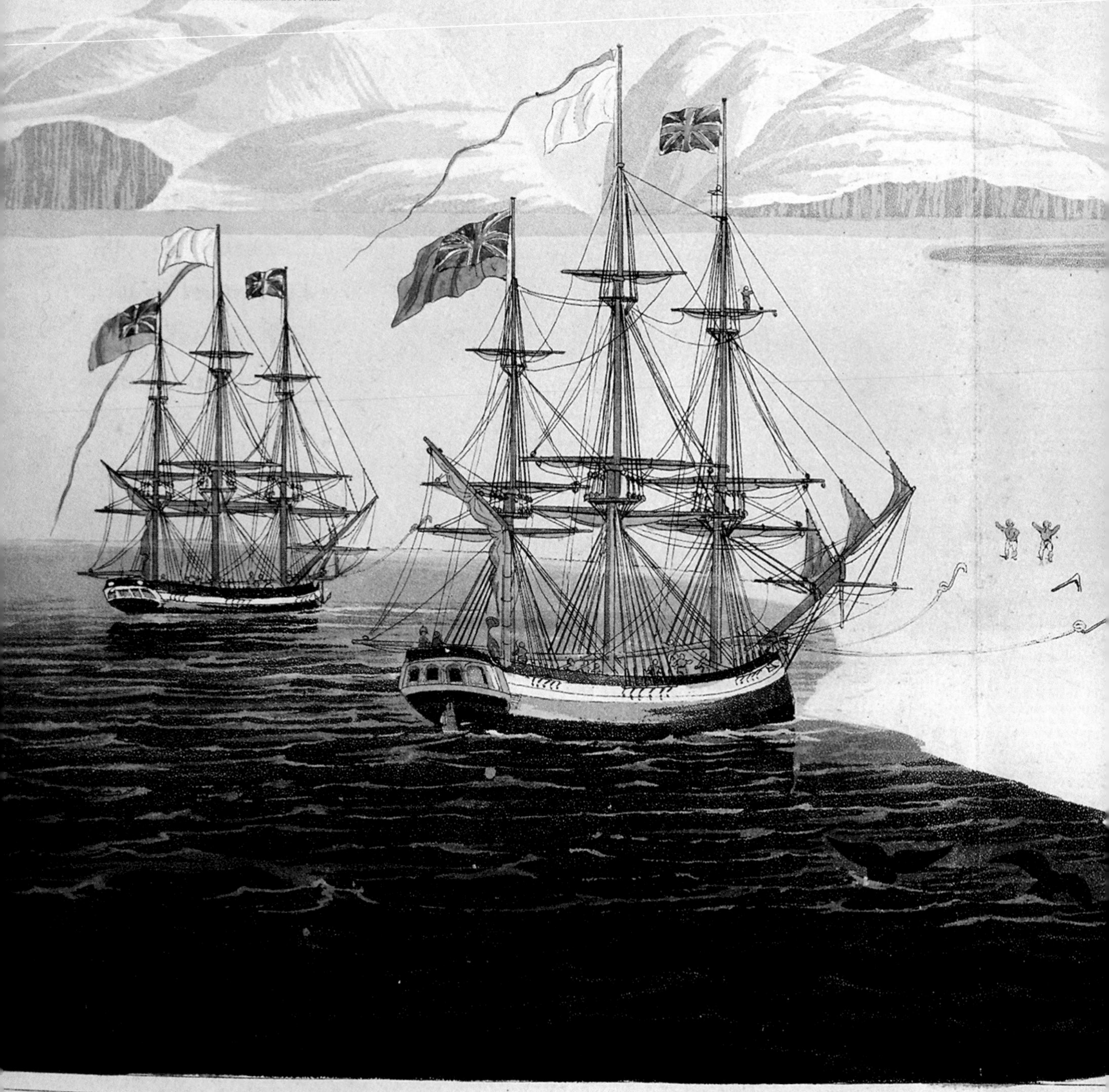

FIRST COMMUNICATION with the NATIVES of PRINCE REGENTS

Drawn by IOHN SACKHEOUSE, and Presented to CAP.T ROSS, Aug.T 10.1818.

One Ocean Voyager, on the first days at sea.

Joseph Frey/*Canadian Geographic*

CHAPTER 3

DESPAIR

E A R L Y   S E P T E M B E R   2 0 1 4 – S E P T E M B E R   7 ,   2 0 1 4

Q U E E N   M A U D   G U L F ,   A R C T I C   O C E A N

RYAN HARRIS AND JONATHAN MOORE, the underwater archaeologists with Parks Canada who had logged the most time searching for Franklin's doomed ships, were astounded. There, on the floor of the Arctic Ocean, viewed through the sonar screen in front of them, was the picture of a ship. They were convinced that it had to be one of Franklin's, either his own, *Erebus,* or its companion, *Terror.* But before anyone in the outside world could know even a whisper about it, they would have to be certain.

They knew two important pieces of information: the only other ship to have been wrecked in this part of the Arctic was a small trading schooner, the *Emma,* in 1932, with few physical similarities to what they were seeing in front of them, and no other navy ship was recorded to have been in these waters. The size and shape of the ship on the screen told them that this was a navy vessel.

Given that the artifacts found on the nearby island were stamped with the arrow marking of the Royal Navy, the odds were strong that they came from the wreck sitting below them on the bottom of the ocean, under only eleven metres of water. But the most telling sign that this was the ship they had been looking for was the peculiar diagonal planking on the ship's deck, visible on the sonar images. This was one of the famous ways the Admiralty had had both *Erebus* and *Terror* structurally strengthened in 1839 to prepare them to withstand the fearsome pressure of the contorting ice.

Harris and the crew of *Investigator* completed approximately twenty more passes with their towfish scanner around and across the top of the sunken ship, trying to record it from every possible angle. Closer and

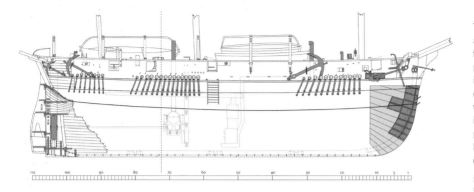

The modifications made to *Erebus* and *Terror* were cutting-edge for their time. They had engines, propellers, heating systems and iron-reinforced bows. The ships' deck planking was modified to better withstand the force of the ice, and it was when Ryan Harris saw this particular modification on sonar that he knew the ship they'd found was one of Franklin's.

BUILDING HMS *TERROR*/BUILDINGTERROR. BLOGSPOT.CA

Side-scan sonar has been around for decades, but it remains an indispensable tool in the search for ship-wrecks. A sonar unit known as a towfish, seen here in the hands of Parks Canada's Ryan Harris and Leading Seaman Yves Bernard of the Royal Canadian Navy, is towed behind a boat via a winch-and-pulley system. The towfish sends out acoustic pings that create a rough image of the sea floor.

closer to the wreck the towfish flew, peering at it with higher and higher concentrations of sound waves. As the waves bounced back up to the towfish, they swiftly filled in a picture of what was below. This was a substantial vessel. They could tell from looking at the length of its shadow that its front end stood upright a full five metres high off the seabed—almost as high as a two-storey building—and the back, more than four.

By that point, they had been able to determine that no masts were rising up from the wreck, and that there was nothing for the towfish and its cable to become tangled in. So then they let the towfish fly right over top, just three metres above the ship. They could see down onto the deck in breathtaking detail. There was a capstan (an upright winch used to wind up heavy rope), the round drum of a windlass (a piece of equipment for raising anchors), part of a pump and a hatch at the front of the ship.

And it was exquisitely, almost unimaginably well preserved. Few of the archaeologists had ever dared dream that they might find one of Franklin's ships so relatively untouched. One of the great fears of the search expeditions over the years was that they might find the ships in a condition they call "toothpicks," just splinters from a once-proud vessel pulverized by the force of the ice. The tiny pieces of the ship would likely have provided some information about how the vessel had been crushed and perhaps where—there might be a trail of debris—but nothing like the prospects for revelation that Harris, Moore, Chriss Ludin and

Side-scan sonar towfish are durable, but if one suffered damage in the Arctic, the year's brief window of open water could disappear as parts for the unit were flown in. Guiding the towfish into the water is a tense affair for the archaeologists, who use extreme caution to ensure it does not come into contact with the stern of the boat on its way in.

TYRONE BURKE/*CANADIAN GEOGRAPHIC*

When archaeologists Ryan Harris (second from left) and Jonathan Moore (second from right) realized they'd discovered the wreck of one of the Franklin expedition's ships, they, along with Marc-André Bernier (third from left), took the unusual step of calling *Sir Wilfrid Laurier*'s captain, Bill Noon (left), into his own quarters for a meeting to share the news.

THERESA NICHOLS/FISHERIES AND OCEANS CANADA/CANADIAN COAST GUARD

Joe Boucher had discovered. Now, for the first time, Harris and Moore could envision going inside the vessel, seeing first-hand where Franklin and his men had walked, possibly finding cherished possessions the men had left behind. It is possible some daguerreotype images, early photographs, had survived in the frigid water and maybe even written records of what went on in those desperate, lethal final months. And maybe, just maybe, there would be answers to some of the intractable mysteries about why the best-prepared expedition the British had ever sent to the Northwest Passage had failed so catastrophically.

They were on the edge of being able to confirm that it was one of Franklin's ships. But before they could do that, Harris would have to inform Marc-André Bernier, chief of Parks Canada's Underwater Archaeology Team, of what they had found. According to a rigid protocol the team had developed in case this day ever arrived, Bernier had to be the one to make the final approval about the ship's authenticity and start the discovery protocol. And at that moment, he was more than a hundred kilometres away, on another ship, locked in the ice, utterly unaware of the spectacular find.

✦

BERNIER WAS ON BOARD *One Ocean Voyager*, one of the group of vessels to be part of the 2014 search for Franklin's ships in Victoria Strait. Originally built in Finland as a Russian ice-strengthened ship, *Akademik Sergey Vavilov*, now it was comfortably refurbished and operated for polar cruises by the private firm One Ocean Expeditions, based in Squamish, B.C.

One Ocean Voyager during the Victoria Strait Expedition.

The 2014 search expedition was the biggest, most expensive, most technically advanced effort in the modern era, an intensive search meticulously planned by Harris with the assistance of tacticians in the Royal Canadian Navy and technical specialists from the other government partners. Bernier had taken to referring to the assembly as "the fleet." However, Bernier, one of about one hundred crew and passengers on *Voyager*, was not searching for Franklin at that crucial moment. Like the others gathered there, he was on standby, waiting for the ice to break up so the team could start looking in the strait.

Victoria Strait is the infamous piece of the Arctic Ocean running down the west side of King William Island. Infamous because, unique in the southerly portion of the Northwest Passage, it is prone to freezing up for years on end, choking as if in the narrow throat of an hourglass between the westernmost point of King William Island and the Royal Geographical Society Islands. This was the remorseless ice that terrified even the hardiest of Victorian Arctic explorers, so murderous that it seemed to take on its own personality. The explorer Francis Leopold McClintock, who went on a series of searches to find Franklin in the 1840s and 1850s, described it in nearly human terms as a tremendous polar pack bred in the Beaufort Sea, as much as fifteen or even twenty-five metres thick, grinding through the ocean to make an impenetrable barrier to ships.[12] Richard Collinson, another who sought Franklin, described it as "a most confused jumble of angular pieces, many of which were upwards of 20 feet [six metres] high."[13]

In late August, as it was becoming clear that ice would prevent the Victoria Strait Expedition from having much access to Victoria Strait, Underwater Archaeology Team chief Marc-André Bernier met with Parks Canada partners on *One Ocean Voyager* to discuss how the team would adapt to evolving conditions.

A rigid-hulled inflatable boat travels toward sea ice, with *One Ocean Voyager* on the horizon.

It was here where Franklin's *Erebus* and her sister ship *Terror* got, as the mariners put it, "beset" in the ice in 1846, after having already spent the first winter of the expedition farther north and then pushing this far south in open water, or at least water not completely choked by ice. Franklin made the disastrous choice of trying to sail down the west side of King William Island instead of down the east side, where the ice offered fewer hazards. His maps showed that the island was connected by a land bridge to the mainland and, therefore, that there was no way for ships to get through but on the west side. After two frustrating winters locked in the frozen wastes, Franklin's surviving 105 men abandoned their ships to the sea and tried to walk south to salvation across the barren King William Island, on their way to Back River (also known as Great Fish River),

In the Arctic, helicopters offer unparalleled mobility to the Coast Guard, and by extension to the scientists hosted on their ships. Able to go farther, faster than ships, and capable of landing almost anywhere, they dramatically extend the Coast Guard's reach in remote areas.

Helicopter pilot Andrew Stirling debriefs Parks Canada and Coast Guard staff on helicopter protocols on board the CCGS *Sir Wilfrid Laurier.*

which in turn would take them to Fort Resolution, a Hudson's Bay Company trading post many hundreds of kilometres farther south. None lived to tell the tale.

For the previous five years, Parks Canada's search for Franklin had been conducted in both a southern search area in the eastern Queen Maud Gulf and a northern area encompassing Alexandra Strait and the southern end of Victoria Strait. The team had pledged that this year, they would muster more forces and extend the search farther north toward the point of abandonment in Victoria Strait, spending as much time as possible there once the ice cleared. They had gathered four ships. First, the navy's coastal defence vessel HMCS *Kingston.* Second, the Canadian Coast Guard icebreaker *Laurier,* which was to be the operational brains for the search and carry Parks Canada's boat *Investigator*—custom built for underwater archaeology and sonar scanning—as well as two survey launches from the Canadian Hydrographic Service, *Kinglett* and *Gannet.* Third, the private Arctic research ship *Martin Bergmann* from the Arctic Research Foundation; and fourth, *Voyager.* As well, two brand-new autonomous underwater vehicles and a remotely operated vehicle were part of the search.

Victoria Strait was the last place Franklin's own crews reported the ships had been, catalogued in a written note found on land in 1859, eleven years after it had been left. There were a few reports in the decades that followed of timbers discovered nearby, some of which may have come from Franklin's ships. They raised the possibility that the ships had been crushed to pieces. But the strait's seabed, which is known to be cruelly riven with ice, had not been completely covered for traces of Franklin's expedition and there was mounting excitement that this year would produce a significant find. Indeed, all search platforms that were to work in the northern search area, in a coordinated fashion, had been assigned individual search blocks by Parks Canada.

While Victoria Strait has frequently been covered in ice over the centuries, it is also one of the most fickle straits in the Arctic and can be ice-free for weeks at a time, as open and placid as a

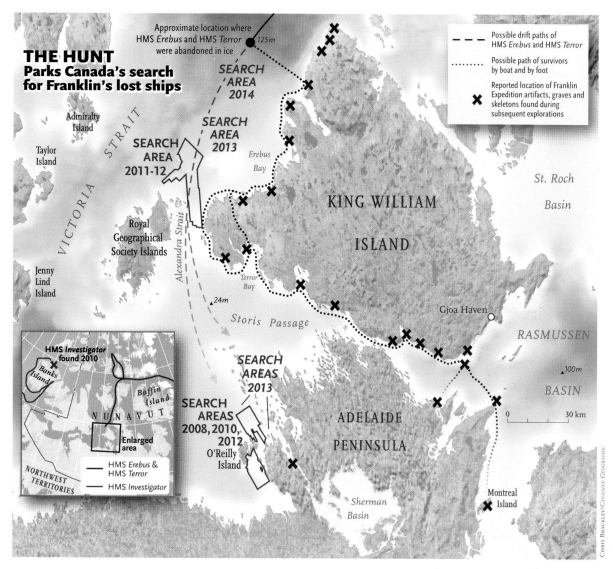

THE HUNT
Parks Canada's search for Franklin's lost ships

Approximate location where HMS *Erebus* and HMS *Terror* were abandoned in ice

SEARCH AREA 2014

SEARCH AREA 2013

SEARCH AREA 2011-12

SEARCH AREAS 2013

SEARCH AREAS 2008, 2010, 2012

- - - Possible drift paths of HMS *Erebus* and HMS *Terror*
.... Possible path of survivors by boat and by foot
✕ Reported location of Franklin Expedition artifacts, graves and skeletons found during subsequent explorations

Admiralty Island

Taylor Island

VICTORIA STRAIT

Erebus Bay

KING WILLIAM ISLAND

St. Roch Basin

Royal Geographical Society Islands

Alexandra Strait

Jenny Lind Island

Terror Bay

24 m

Storis Passage

Gjoa Haven

RASMUSSEN BASIN

100 m

O'Reilly Island

ADELAIDE PENINSULA

Montreal Island

Sherman Basin

0   30 km

HMS *Investigator* found 2010

Banks Island

Baffin Island

N U N A V U T

Enlarged area

NORTHWEST TERRITORIES

—— HMS *Erebus* & HMS *Terror*
—— HMS *Investigator*

CHRIS BRACKLEY/CANADIAN GEOGRAPHIC

Parks Canada's archaeologists work around the clock when weather permits, but the overwhelming majority of Queen Maud Gulf and Victoria Strait remains unsurveyed. Prioritizing areas where a find is probable is necessary. Such areas are chosen based on Inuit testimony, tips from local people about possible artifacts they've spotted, ice dynamics, likely drift patterns, and of course weather. Many of the areas highlighted here are near harbours that provide shelter in high winds.

southern lake. So this year, not only was Victoria Strait targeted, but it had also, bravely, given its name to the summer's quest: the Victoria Strait Expedition.

And they were there, poised for action, right near the storied point in the strait where Franklin's crew had abandoned the ships 166 years earlier. It was profoundly moving to be in that location, where that fateful decision was made with such horrifying consequences.

But, frustratingly, the ice had again come back to the strait, against all hope. It was new ice, unlike the

The well deck of CCGS *Sir Wilfrid Laurier* is the crowded hub of its operations. Here, boats from Parks Canada, the Canadian Hydrographic Service and the Canadian Coast Guard all vie for deck space.

The Victoria Strait Expedition brought an unprecedented number of private sector partners to Parks Canada's search. Among the partners are Jim Balsillie of the Arctic Research Foundation, Geordie Dalglish of The W. Garfield Weston Foundation, and John Geiger and André Préfontaine of The Royal Canadian Geographical Society.

The Arctic demands ingenuity and self-reliance of all who venture there. The Coast Guard's Keith Graham (right) is one of those who embody this spirit. Seen here piloting a Canadian Hydrographic Service boat as it charts the ocean floor with multibeam sonar, the leading seaman also later built the protective crate used to safely transport *Erebus*'s bell to Ottawa.

material that lasted for years in Franklin's day, the pitilessly hard substance called multi-year ice. Nonetheless, it was plentiful and persistent. Day after day, at 4:00 p.m. sharp, Bernier and the team anxiously waited for the Canadian Ice Service charts that would tell them where the ice was and how much, and whether a strong wind would blow enough of it away that the search could finally begin. The charts work by percentage, coded to colour. Red indicates 90 per cent to 100 per cent ice coverage in the strait. Orange indicates 70 per cent to 80 per cent ice coverage. In order for the search to proceed safely, the coverage needed to be zero.

Day after day, the charts came in red and orange. It was by far the worst ice any Parks Canada search had seen in years. And to add to the misery, the quality of the ice was poor, a condition known as "rotten" ice, which meant it was close to falling to pieces. Each day, the ice was tantalizingly close to being swept away. Or, if it disintegrated enough, the ships, laden with all their high-tech gear and dozens of scientists, financial donors and observers, might have been able to sail through. But that didn't happen. Instead it was a cat-and-mouse game. Everyone was on tenterhooks.

THIS EXPEDITION HAD BEEN more than a year in the making, the culmination of a fever to find Franklin's ships that had been growing in Canada for three decades. One of the people who has felt the Arctic passion keenly is Stephen Harper, who as prime minister revealed himself to be a devout polar enthusiast. He has made a ritual pilgrimage to the North each summer and has even been known to camp out on the land there, dreaming under the starry skies.

The Arctic is highly symbolic to the prime minister, just as it was to his Victorian predecessors. To him, it is the seat of Canada's sovereignty, the last great uncharted piece of the country,

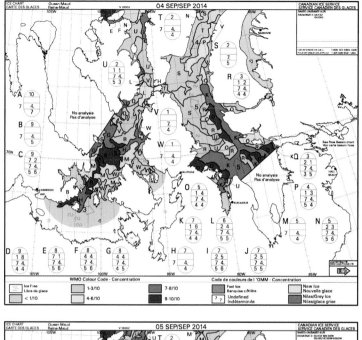

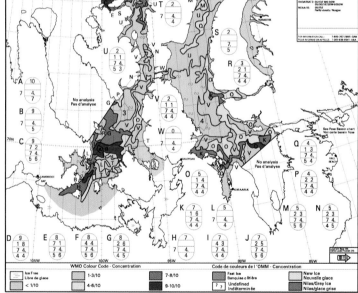

With red areas indicating ice cover of over 90 percent and blue ones indicating less than 10 percent, the colour-coded charts produced each day by the Canadian Ice Service helped Parks Canada's archaeologists adapt their search strategy to ever-changing ice conditions.

the piece that is critical to its identity, its mineral and fishing and possession rights over the continental shelf off Canada's northern coast.

It may even be a key to its future prosperity in ways unimaginable in years past. Harper is all too aware that, by a twist of fate, the ice-fast Northwest Passage that defeated Franklin will soon be melted enough to be the reliable trade route Franklin sought. It may even open up enough to present the possibilities of tourism, mining and oil and gas exploration. The changing nature of the Arctic has fascinated him throughout his prime ministership.

To him, the fascination coalesces in the Northwest Passage and in Franklin. As he has said many times, the story of the Arctic, and more particularly, of the Northwest Passage, is the story of Canada itself. The giants of his country's history, the men who first explored Canada and who therefore helped to give birth to it, also attempted the Northwest Passage.

Among those early Arctic explorers, Franklin has a special place in Harper's heart. For one thing, the story has been a profound and enduring mystery that teases the imagination. But it runs deeper than that. Franklin has come to represent the spirit of the Canada that Harper admires. He sees Franklin as a proxy for the daring, uninhibited, heroic Canadian—one who sails boldly

With a background in the tech industry, entrepreneur and philanthropist Jim Balsillie set his sights on the North, co-founding an NGO with fellow businessman Tim MacDonald. The Arctic Research Foundation was the first non-governmental entity to partner in the search for Franklin.

into impossibly unforgiving territory, not knowing if success is even possible, not caring what it costs him, willing to risk everything in the hope of great reward. It is the story of these modern-day Franklin explorers, and, some would say, of Harper too, a leader who fashioned political power from the risky marriage of two parties and held on to it.

Jim Balsillie is one of the powerhouses behind the search and, some would say, the search's secret weapon. Balsillie, who helped found the Canadian telecommunication and wireless technology company Research In Motion (now BlackBerry), became gripped by the Arctic in 2008, drawn by what he calls its "unbelievable power and beauty." Now a philanthropist who has retired from the company, he has said that he has put millions of dollars into the Arctic Research Foundation he helped to found.

He can pinpoint the moment that the momentum for the 2014 find began to build. It was 2010 and he and his foundation's co-founder, Tim MacDonald, were at a meeting in Ottawa's tony Rideau Club—seat of the business, civil service and political elite—with Andrew Campbell, the Canadian government's executive responsible for the search, Bernier and Harris. Balsillie asked Campbell what it would take to find Franklin's ships. Campbell said, "We need a boat!" Balsillie responded, "Okay. Done."

The problem, as Balsillie identified it, was that Parks Canada needed a small and nimble ship, not a heavy icebreaker, that was theirs alone, outfitted with sonar and crew, so they could make maximum use of the narrow window of search time available each summer. That's when his foundation bought a nineteen-metre vessel and outfitted it especially for the search. The vessel was renamed *Martin Bergmann* after Balsillie's Arctic mentor, the head of the Polar Continental Shelf Program, who died in an airplane crash in 2011.

To Balsillie, the seabed search area was like a giant jigsaw puzzle. It was a case of methodically removing the pieces where Franklin's ships could not be.

The *Martin Bergmann* can search as much as 370 square kilometres of seabed a year. With the boat and dedicated search time it could provide, Balsillie believed that finding Franklin's ships was just a matter of time.

"I thought, if they're there, we'll find them. If it's ten years or twenty, so be it," he said.

And the *Martin Bergmann* has been an undisputed workhorse of the search for Franklin ever since.

Balsillie has nurtured the mission quietly behind the scenes, marshalling its components until it became bigger and then wildly successful. His image is of a snowball gradually getting bigger and bigger, gaining strength and speed until it is unstoppable.

To Balsillie, the story of the Arctic is a key element of Canada's narrative. And to him, the search for

Before Jim Balsillie brought the MV *Martin Bergmann* north to Cambridge Bay, there was no ship dedicated to the search for *Erebus* and *Terror*. Parks Canada's searchers worked from Coast Guard ships and around Coast Guard priorities, such as search and rescue. Having a dedicated ship allowed archaeologists to target areas Inuit testimony indicated were of highest probability for a find.

NICK WALKER/*CANADIAN GEOGRAPHIC*

Franklin is enmeshed in that. It is, Balsillie believes, the foundation of a powerful new national narrative. Finding Franklin is to Canada what sending Franklin off to find the Northwest Passage was to Britain in 1845. It is Canada's birthright. Balsillie can draw a direct line between the elements that characterize this modern quest and those at play when Franklin set out: geopolitics, Arctic sovereignty, the frontiers of science and technology, climate, weather, mystery, ambition.

When he became involved, Balsillie knew that searchers from other countries had also been trying to find the lost ships and that troubled him deeply. He was not going to sit idly by while another nation tried to claim what he saw as Canada's due. To that end, he said, his partnership agreement with the Canadian government explicitly states that all players in the search must be Canadian. To him, finding Franklin would reinforce Canada in the national psyche as a polar nation.

Balsillie also has a passion for the Royal Canadian Navy—he is an honorary navy captain for the Arctic—and he dreamed of involving the navy in the search as well. So in 2013, he had dinner with Rear Admiral John Newton and invited him to put navy crewmen on the *Martin Bergmann*.

Newton, who has three commands, each of which intersects with the eastern part of the Arctic, was moved by what he calls Balsillie's "passionate search." It sparked memories of the month-long voy-

PMO/Jason Ransom

The flag of The Royal Canadian Geographical Society flew on HMCS *Kingston*, held up by the partners of the expedition, including (top, left to right) Geordie Dalglish of The W. Garfield Weston Foundation, André Préfontaine of The Royal Canadian Geographical Society, Capt. Paul Smith of HMCS *Kingston*, Prime Minister Stephen Harper, John Geiger of The Royal Canadian Geographical Society, Jim Balsillie of the Arctic Research Foundation, and (bottom, left to right) Andrew Prossin of One Ocean Expeditions and Environment Minister Leona Aglukkaq. The photo was taken at Pond Inlet.

age Newton took at fourteen, tracing part of Franklin's route in the Arctic on HMCS *Protecteur*. That voyage in 1973 ignited Newton's lifelong love of the Arctic—and, indeed, planted the seeds of his navy career—and when he got home from the dinner with Balsillie, he pulled out the photo album from that trip, savouring his Franklin memories. He decided to provide a side-scan sonar assistant, a cook and a boatswain for the *Martin Bergmann* that year.

By 2014, as the team grew, the navy became much more intimately involved, putting, as Newton said, the "whole weight" of the navy behind the mission. He provided the services of one of his own highly skilled operational planning staff, and the mission built in crucial tests of the *Arctic Explorer*, an autonomous underwater vehicle equipped with state-of-the-art synthetic aperture sonar developed by Kraken Sonar, a Canadian company based in Newfoundland. The vehicle was capable of searching for the wrecks and also mapping the ocean floor with superb precision, as well as performing military tasks.

Shortly thereafter, The Royal Canadian Geographical Society joined the coalition of searchers. The society had been founded in 1929 to pick up the mantle in Canada of Britain's storied Royal Geographical Society,

Stephen Harper and his wife, Laureen, at a campfire near Gjoa Haven, Nunavut, during the prime minister's 2013 northern tour.

which had been a driver of the search for the Northwest Passage and subsequently the search to ascertain the fate of Franklin. At the Canadian society's inaugural meeting, Sir Francis Younghusband, an explorer and past-president of The Royal Geographical Society, presented a ceremonial sword from the king of Bhutan to Charles Camsell, the founding president, himself an explorer and one-time commissioner of the Northwest Territories. This act symbolized the inheritance by the young society of a tradition of supporting exploration.

In August 2013, John Geiger, in his capacity as chief executive officer of The Royal Canadian Geographical Society, participated in the prime minister's annual northern tour, travelling on Royal Canadian Air Force 001 to Whitehorse, Yukon, then by Hercules fixed-wing turboprop aircraft across the Arctic, with stops in places like Rankin Inlet, Nunavut. At one point, they landed at Gjoa Haven, on King William Island. That night, after practising their shots with Lee-Enfield rifles and meeting with the Canadian Rangers, they camped on the tundra, more than thirty kilometres from the hamlet. Around an enormous bonfire built by the rangers, on the island where so many of Franklin's men had died, the prime minister and Geiger spoke about the Franklin problem, the frustration that no ships had been found, the mystery and grotesque nature of the expedition's end.

Ryan Harris gives Environment Minister Leona Aglukkaq a hand as she pilots a Parks Canada remotely operated vehicle during an equipment demonstration aboard HMCS *Kingston* in Pond Inlet, Nunavut. It was this particular remotely operated vehicle that later made the first dive to *Erebus* on September 7, 2015.

JONATHAN MOORE/PARKS CANADA

Ryan Harris shows Environment Minister Leona Aglukkaq and Prime Minister Stephen Harper Parks Canada's nimble Iver3 autonomous underwater vehicle (equipped with side-scan sonar, among other instruments) in Pond Inlet.

JONATHAN MOORE/PARKS CANADA

The prime minister struck Geiger as having more than a layman's interest in the subject, no doubt inspired by his sincere passion for the Arctic. It was an amazing experience, huddled around the fire, with Environment Minister (and Gjoa Haven native) Leona Aglukkaq, Chief of the Defence Staff General Thomas Lawson, the prime minister's wife, Laureen Harper, and others nearby, talking Franklin. At their backs lurked a biting and intense cold, and eventually, as the summer twilight slipped into night, absolute darkness.

The next day, they travelled by small boat back to Gjoa Haven and then out to rendezvous with the *Laurier*. On board, Harris, the underwater archaeologist, briefed the prime minister about that year's search. Surveying would continue in Queen Maud Gulf, where Inuit testimony had placed one of the wrecks, and the Parks Canada team and its partners would continue to survey in Alexandra Strait and Victoria Strait, where the other ship was supposed to have sunk. Douglas Stenton, the Nunavut archaeologist, filled the prime minister in on the land-based component of the Franklin search. The conversation focused on a map of the central Arctic.

Franklin and many of the earlier generations of searchers had hand-drawn maps, imperfect compasses and incomplete understandings of both the land and the ice. As Newton said, they didn't always know where the next piece of land was or where the bottom rose. Today, searchers have satellite pictures from space to predict the flow of ice and sonar systems that help them avoid obstacles in uncharted waters.

By that fall of 2013, when it came time for the speech from the throne, which sets out the government's intentions for its year's work, the government pledged "renewed determination" to discover Franklin's fate, along with an expanded roster of partners.

Soon the geographical society joined the partnership led by Parks Canada, its government partners and the Arctic

Research Foundation. The society's efforts were focused on telling the story of the search to the broad public through its magazine, *Canadian Geographic*, and to schoolchildren through its network of fifteen thousand classroom educators, Canadian Geographic Education. These efforts were supported by an additional team of Canada's exploration leaders, including some of the champions of Canadian industry, among them The W. Garfield Weston Foundation, which has heavily supported scientific research in the Arctic for years; One Ocean Expeditions, which operates polar adventure expeditions and helps educate about the Arctic; and Shell Canada, whose parent company has been looking for oil in the Arctic since 1917 and has been a strong advocate for geographic education. Together, this partnership also contributed *One Ocean Voyager*, which additionally served as a platform to support the research.

And of course, there was Balsillie. Geiger first met him at a hotel in Ottawa, at a meeting with Campbell and Parks Canada chief executive officer Alan Latourelle. Balsillie was gracious and welcoming. He was also tenacious, with his drive now focused on the search for Franklin's ships. The Arctic Research Foundation had already made a substantial impact, with the research vessel *Martin Bergmann* helping to dramatically increase the coverage achieved by the Parks Canada search efforts. Balsillie also supported the society's outreach efforts, convinced of the importance of building public interest in and knowledge of Canada's Arctic. The expanded partnership sought a success for the country that would shape the way Canadians see themselves and the way others see Canadians. They saw the search for Franklin as the unmatched opportunity of a generation, a quest that required both passion and vision.

✦

THE PRESSURE TO SUCCEED was immense. The equipment and vessels were assembled; the partners were gathered; the public was anxiously awaiting results. And just after the 2014 search season had begun, the prime minister made his annual visit to the Arctic. On the bridge of the navy vessel *Kingston* at Pond Inlet, on the northeastern side of Nunavut's Baffin Island, he congratulated all the modern explorers and partners, some of whom were there gathered on board with him. Among those assembled were Aglukkaq, whose Environment Ministry takes in Parks Canada; Balsillie; Geordie Dalglish, northern committee chair of The W. Garfield Weston Foundation; One Ocean Expedition's managing director and veteran polar tour leader Andrew Prossin; Harris and Moore of Parks Canada; Glenn Toldi of the Canadian Hydrographic Service; and André Préfontaine and Geiger, representing The Royal Canadian Geographical Society. Those assembled joined Newton in reciting the prayer for Her Majesty's Canadian Navy ("O Eternal Lord God, who alone spreadest out the heavens, and rulest the raging of the sea; who has compassed the waters with bounds until day and night come to an end . . ."). With that, the prime minister raised a glass of Scotch whisky and toasted Franklin's memory, averring that this would be the year to find the explorer.

Eclipse Sound has the sort of scenery Arctic dreams are made of, and it was here, just off the coast of Baffin Island at Pond Inlet, that the partners of the Victoria Strait Expedition, on board HMCS *Kingston* during the early days of the expedition, toasted the dream of finding one of Franklin's lost ships.

MICHELLE VALBERG

Ships on the water, including HMCS *Kingston*, as night falls over Pond Inlet.

The search for *Erebus* and *Terror* has focused on two general areas. In the south, Inuit testimony told of a ship in Queen Maud Gulf, not far from the Adelaide Peninsula, where HMS *Erebus* was found. To the north, the focus is in Victoria Strait, where a ship was abandoned in the ice, and where HMS *Terror* might yet be found.

CHRIS BRACKLEY/*CANADIAN GEOGRAPHIC*

Nobody wanted to disappoint Harper or dash the renewed hopes of the public or the investors. And yet not long after that, the team was gathered in Victoria Strait, prepared to search but not searching. Blocked by the ice. Things had begun to unravel for the search in Victoria Strait within days of the toast on the bridge.

First, the navy vessel *Kingston* was forced to delay and eventually abandon its participation in Victoria Strait because there was too much ice. *Voyager* doubled back to meet it in order to retrieve crates of equipment for the search, including the remotely operated vehicle.

Voyager was already carrying the most sophisticated piece of equipment ever sent to find Franklin: *Arctic Explorer*, a giant, canary-yellow autonomous underwater vehicle developed for mine hunting by International Submarine Engineering, a firm based in Coquitlam, B.C., and outfitted with an acoustic homing system developed by Nova Scotia's Omnitech. Its synthetic aperture sonar—the latest technology—was designed by another Canadian technology leader, Kraken Sonar, to make crystal-clear images of the ocean floor using

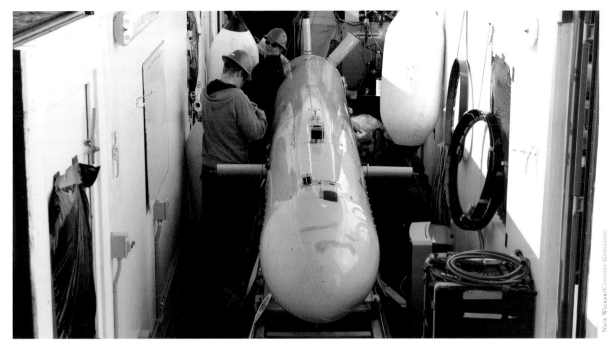

An autonomous underwater vehicle (AUV) first joined the search for Franklin in 2012. The deployment of Defence Research and Development Canada's *Arctic Explorer* AUV (shown here in its storage container) during the Victoria Strait Expedition added a highly sophisticated and capable vehicle to the search.

Defence Research and Development Canada staff guide the *Arctic Explorer* AUV into its storage container on the deck of *One Ocean Voyager*.

Developed in St. John's, Newfoundland, the synthetic aperture sonar used by *Arctic Explorer* uses sophisticated post-processing of sonar information to create a high-resolution image of the ocean floor.

sound waves, scanning three hundred metres on either side of itself. It was the first time that this type of sonar equipment was to be used in the Canadian Arctic. Newton said it is capable of giving more precise information than any other sonar equipment in the Arctic Ocean. It would be able to pick up even small shards of a ship's wreck on the bottom of the sea, he said. As well, it can be in the water searching on its own for days at a time, then find its way back to the ship that launched it. Some members of the search team were heavily anticipating that this vehicle would be the one to make the year's breakthrough. Because of its capacity, it had been given the research block in the central axis of the projected trajectory from the point of abandonment of Franklin's ships.

There were other expectations for *Arctic Explorer*. Newton and others in the navy were also keen to see how the vehicle's digital compass would react this close to the magnetic North Pole, and they wanted to see generally how it would perform in the region. Modern navy vessels in the Arctic need to be equipped to support hydrography, fisheries, security, mapping, commercial interests and military interests, and the underwater vehicle may eventually be able to serve in some of those areas, Newton said.

Here, too, the ice was playing havoc with the plans. The team at Defence Research and Development Canada, an agency of the Canadian government, was keen to test its new high-grade sonar system for its first foray in the Canadian Arctic. But the ice refused to budge. Occasionally, a small opening, or lead, would appear in the ice, and Richard Pederson, in charge of autonomous underwater vehicle systems for Defence Research and Development Canada in the Atlantic, would launch *Arctic Explorer*. It was an amazing sight, this yellow torpedo that would swim off on its own, carrying out its mission followed by several inflatable vessels full of searchers, Bernier among them, before it would dive from view. But then, only hours into its mission, ice would gather where there had been water and the team would pull the vehicle back before it got trapped under the ice. It was agonizing. The team went through these extremes of elation and then of exasperation, as it was deployed and then recalled.

Deployed from the deck of *One Ocean Voyager*, *Arctic Explorer* was secured by Royal Canadian Navy personnel around the clock throughout the Victoria Strait Expedition.

As the search extends farther north in Victoria Strait into deeper water, making towed side-scan sonar searching difficult, archaeologists can turn to other methods, such as multibeam sonar systems and autonomous underwater vehicles like the *Arctic Explorer*.

Arctic Explorer derives from the *Explorer* AUV, both of which were designed and built by International Submarine Engineering of British Columbia.

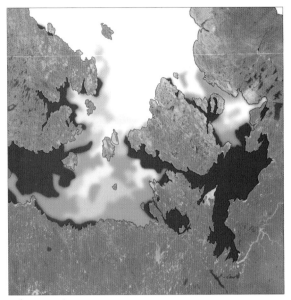

AUGUST 6

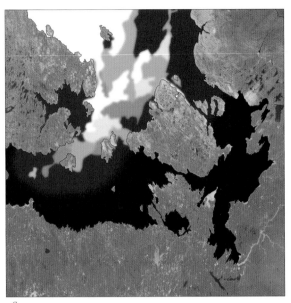

SEPTEMBER 9

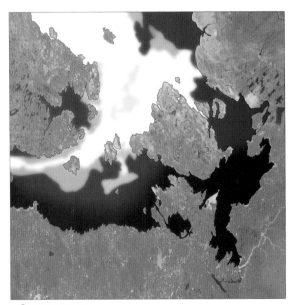

SEPTEMBER 22

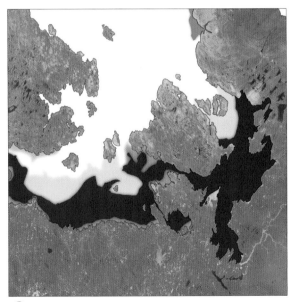

OCTOBER 2

Ice movement in Victoria Strait over the course of eight weeks in 2014.

And it wasn't assigned to be deployed farther south, where the ice had already melted, because the side-scan and multibeam sonar of the smaller vessels was more ideally suited to those shallow waters and the *Voyager* could not travel there for navigation and safety reasons. This ten-million-dollar piece of equipment, the most sophisticated equipment for finding Franklin in the northern area, was mothballed for the moment.

Pederson said it called to mind the hardships Franklin and his men had gone through. "You can have all the greatest, most technologically advanced equipment available, and you are still at the mercy of the environment," he said.

And it got worse. *Martin Bergmann*, the boat Balsillie had outfitted, covering to date more seabed than all the other vessels combined, is not an ice-rated vessel, so it couldn't shift to the search area near Victoria Strait. *Laurier* could be in the ice, but the three smaller launches that do the bulk of its searching, *Investigator*, *Gannet* and *Kinglett*, could not.

All this equipment, all these high-powered partners, their drive to get this search underway, even the blessing of the prime minister—and little could be done in the northern search area. The ice ruled against it and the ice could not be persuaded otherwise.

✦

MEANWHILE, *LAURIER*, along with the Parks Canada boat *Investigator* and the Canadian Hydrographic Service launches *Gannet* and *Kinglett*, as well as the *Martin Bergmann*, was in the ice-free waters of Queen Maud Gulf, where this combined team had worked in earlier years, following the lead of David Woodman, the Franklin scholar who has intensively studied Inuit testimony and who first identified the more southerly search area. The plan was that when the ice farther north in Victoria Strait cleared, they could move there and help with that part of the search. Here in the gulf, they were using a proven search technology: side-scan sonars with a remotely operated vehicle on hand in case they ended up needing it and a small, but highly capable, autonomous underwater vehicle.

But all of a sudden, Bernier, cooling his heels on *Voyager*, locked in a wait-and-see game with the ice, deploying *Arctic Explorer* and then aborting each mission and calling the high-tech gear home, was summoned by satellite phone. He was asked to get to the *Laurier*. By sheer luck, another Canadian Coast Guard icebreaker, CCGS *Pierre Radisson*, was nearby, and Bernier boarded a Zodiac that whisked him over to it. Without the icebreaker's help, he might have had no way to join the team before *Voyager* had to return to Cambridge Bay at the end of its participation in the expedition. Then it was onto the *Radisson*'s helicopter and over to meet Harris, Moore and the rest of the team on *Laurier* in Alexandra Strait. (The *Laurier* had moved north and had spent three productive days surveying in this area dodging ice floes and working along the ice edge. Douglas Stenton and his colleague Robert Park, whose plans for terrestrial archaeological work on King William Island had also been curtailed by the ice in Victoria Strait, were able to get ashore. There,

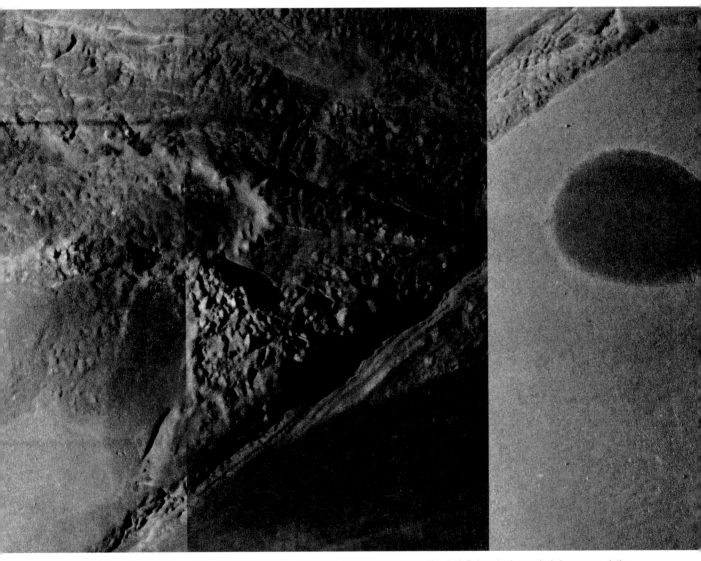

Synthetic aperture sonar images of the seabed in Victoria Strait, collected by the autonomous underwater vehicle *Arctic Explorer*, showing massive iceberg scours and other interesting sea floor features.

Underwater Archaeology Team leader Marc-André Bernier rushed away from *One Ocean Voyager*, first by Zodiac to CCGS *Radisson*, to join other members of the team in the southern search area, not yet knowing that *Erebus* had been found.

The helicopter sent to retrieve Parks Canada's Marc-André Bernier from *One Ocean Voyager* lands on the flight deck of nearby CCGS *Pierre Radisson*.

they reinterred human remains of Franklin expedition members they had excavated the year before on the shores of Erebus Bay and had studied intensively in the intervening time.)

When Bernier saw what they had found, the tears began to well up in his eyes. Bill Noon, captain of the *Laurier*, was also let in on the secret, as was Stenton. Noon began to cry freely. After all the frustration that the ice in Victoria Strait had caused that year, keeping the search to the south, the find seemed fated. "Somebody was pushing us to an answer," Noon said. "Somebody had waited long enough and wanted to solve the riddle."

Like the few others who knew about the find, Harris and Bernier were confident that this really was one of Franklin's ships. But they needed to send the remotely operated vehicle (ROV), akin to an underwater robot—the one rescued from *Kingston* when the ice forced it to postpone the mission—into the ocean to take video before they could alert the world, in accordance with a predetermined protocol that was followed to the letter. The *Laurier* started to head back south to the wreck and the combined team set about reconfiguring *Investigator* for a planned ROV dive.

It was dreadful weather for taking underwater video. Huge winds whipped the ocean up into waves that reached three or four metres on the way south. The choppy water was murky and the wreck itself was obscured with seaweed. But finally the Parks Canada team got the first ever image of the wreck, and then there was no question. The ship was in immaculate condition. It was heart-rendingly beautiful. By its appearance, and by the fact that they could see Royal Navy's brass cannons, they knew for certain it was one of Franklin's.

At 7:00 p.m., September 7, 2014, Eastern Standard Time, Bernier made the official confirmation, setting the stage for the announcement that one of Franklin's ships had been found after 166 years of searching. He, Harris, Moore, Noon and Stenton knew that the news would dominate international headlines, and that these first images of what would come to be known to be *Erebus* in her last resting place would rivet people all around the world.

A 1905 illustration by A.S. Forrest depicts *Erebus* and *Terror* locked in the ice in 1847. As there are no mountains on King William Island, the artist seems to have taken licence in imagining the scene.

CHAPTER 4

PRISONERS OF ICE

SEPTEMBER 12, 1846 – APRIL 26, 1848

OFF KING WILLIAM ISLAND, ARCTIC OCEAN

AT FIRST, BEING LOCKED in the ice in Victoria Strait was business as usual for Sir John Franklin and his men. It was to be expected in the Arctic. It was one of the reasons Franklin's two ships, *Erebus* and *Terror*, had been so solidly reinforced to withstand the power of buckling ice. It was also why they had the unusual provision of heated berths, not to mention three years' worth of food, much of it tinned.

In fact, the expedition had reason to feel chuffed. The first year of Franklin's mission to claim the Northwest Passage for Britain had gone well. Franklin left Greenland in the summer of 1845, sailed west through Lancaster Sound, south of Devon Island, and then, venturing north through the Wellington Channel, became the first European to explore it. He completed that first phase of the expedition by sailing in a loop around Cornwallis Island, reaching the impressive northern latitude of 77 degrees, which was a feat not to be repeated for more than half a century. Modern analysis shows that the ice must have been unusually open that year for Franklin's wooden Victorian ships to have accomplished such a journey, Thomas Zagon of the Canadian Ice Service has said.

Then Franklin took shelter for the winter in a bay next to Beechey Island, a tiny, desolate islet just southwest of the bulk of Devon Island. It is not very far inside the eastern mouth of the Northwest Passage and is several hundred kilometres northeast of Victoria Strait. Naturally, the bay froze over in the winter. As they expected, the men set up a rather intricate winter camp on the island, establishing tents, a forge and a carpenter's shop. They took geomagnetic observations, as they had promised Sir Edward Sabine they

HMS *Erebus* and HMS *Terror* in the ice at Beechey Island in the winter of 1845–46.

would do. They also neatly arranged six hundred emptied food tins and filled them with stones to create a cairn.

As well, they constructed the carefully marked, beautifully detailed graves of the first three men to die on the expedition—John Torrington, John Hartnell and William Braine—each of whom perished in the first third of 1846. Modern autopsies of these three men, in research led by Owen Beattie, shows that they died of pneumonia, suffered from tuberculosis and, disturbingly, had unusually high levels of lead in their bodies when they died.

Once the ice cleared later that year—again, unusually early—Franklin's ships moved south and west toward King William Island and Victoria Strait, avoiding the eastern side of the island because the charts of the day showed it was connected to the mainland.

But, in late summer, not too far off the northwest tip of King William Island at the top of Victoria Strait, the unforgiving ice caught them and refused to let go, trapping both ships the same day, September 12, 1846. Zagon has said the only explanation is that a ferocious Arctic storm instantly, unluckily and suddenly closed up the ice floes they were navigating through. If the storm had hit a day or two earlier or later,

Canned food was a new concept when the Franklin expedition brought it into the Arctic in 1845, but it became an important source of sustenance for later explorers. Discarded cans on Beechey Island are frequently mistaken for cans left by Franklin and his men, but more often they're associated with subsequent expeditions.

High in the Arctic, the Beechey Island site where the Franklin expedition spent their first winter is desolate. This was where the first three members of the expedition perished, and to beautify their burial site the crew made seashell arrangements on the men's graves.

The cold, dry environment of the High Arctic preserved the bodies buried on Beechey Island. Their lifelike—if frostbitten—appearance shocked the public when forensic anthropological study of their remains was done by Owen Beattie in the 1980s.

Franklin might have made it through. More unluckily, the ships were caught on the eastern side of Victoria Strait, at a point where the ice moves south extraordinarily slowly, holding the potential for ships to be trapped for years on end. If the ships had sailed slightly more to the west within the strait, they might have eventually been carried through.

Franklin and his crew would have been unaware of the layers of bad luck they had encountered. Franklin might have preferred to have been sheltered in a bay rather than out in the open ocean, surrounded by thick, moving ice, but he likely found his situation manageable, if dangerous. Being trapped in heavy ice carries a constant threat of damage if winds or currents shift just the wrong way. By May the following year—1847—a group of two officers and six men were sent off the ships to King William Island. That information was contained in two copies of the same note deposited at two different points on the island, one of which was a stone cairn at Victory Point. Found more than a decade after it was left, it declared, "All well."

It is believed based on later discoveries that at some point early in their besetment, Franklin or one of the other leaders also ordered a magnetic observatory set up at Cape Felix, the most northern tip of King William Island; perhaps the foray described in the Victory Cairn note was in aid of that project. This was precisely what Franklin had been ordered to do, and the early evidence suggested he was following that plan to the letter. At that point, the expedition was not in disarray.

What was life like early on for the men imprisoned on the ice in those ships? The Victory

Point cairn note with its later additions is the only written record. It indicated that things were running smoothly, despite evidence from the Beechey Island graves that illness was already at play among the men on the ships. But a few hints survive in Inuit accounts gathered in the late 1860s by the eccentric American explorer Charles Francis Hall. He lived with the Inuit for five years, obsessed with discerning and recording what they knew about Franklin's fate. Hall's chronicles, along with Inuit accounts given to some of Franklin's other would-be rescuers, were analyzed in David Woodman's 1991 book *Unravelling the Franklin Mystery: Inuit Testimony.*

The Inuit told Hall that some of them had visited two ships beset in the ice on the west side of King William Island.[14] One of the men, Kokleearngnun, showed Hall two silver spoons stamped with the initials of Francis R.M. Crozier, captain of *Terror*, which he said he had received from a man on the ship. His wife, Koonarng, had a silver watch case. Kokleearngnun told Hall that he had set up tents and lived beside the ships on the ice for a time. He described a great, communal caribou hunt with both Inuit and European participants. The latter used guns and knives with long handles.

Intriguingly, he told Hall that they had been on the ships, describing a jovial commander, a thickly proportioned, bald and bespectacled man who offered them food. "He was a cheerful man, always laughing; everybody liked him—all the kob-lu-nas [white men] and all the Innuits [*sic*]."[15] The last time they saw him, he seemed sick and he was lame.

Woodman could not say, as perhaps no historian can, whether Kokleearngnun and Koonarng were describing visits to *Erebus* and *Terror*. He concluded that the Inuit had such detailed knowledge of the ships and men that they had certainly come in contact either with Franklin's ships or with those of another explorer, likely John Ross, or both. Ross's ship *Victory* was locked in the ice for four winters in the early 1830s on the eastern side of Boothia Peninsula, a fat thumb of the continent that sticks up from the coast directly east of King William Island. Ross made a daring and remarkable escape back to Britain. Ross, however, was known to be an irascible captain with a luxuriant head of hair, and his expedition had a single captain rather than the two Kokleearngnun described. That suggests Kokleearngnun might have been on Franklin's ship.

The accounts that Hall heard from Inuit who were on King William Island may furnish a few fascinating clues about the early days of the expedition's imprisonment in the ice. For one thing, they give the impression that Inuit, though perhaps few, were monitoring European ships that came into the Arctic. Inuit were an intriguing and watchful presence, even if mainly unacknowledged by Franklin's crew, rather than an utter absence. Franklin's men were not all alone in the snowy wilderness.

For another, if Kokleearngnun and Koonarng were describing Franklin, they drew the picture of an easygoing group of sailors on two highly functioning ships. This was not a picture of distress or mayhem or fear. Not only that, but if, as they said, the captain was sick and lame, then that added weight to the theory that Franklin may have died in his bed of illness, rather than by any other mishap. Historians have long wondered about his precise cause of death, because no written record exists and no body has been found so far.

The date of his death, however, is clear. An addendum to Fitzjames's note recorded Franklin's death on June 11, 1847, nearly two years after he sailed down the Thames in *Erebus* with such high hopes for redemption.

The mystique of the Franklin expedition transcended the borders of the British Empire. The Ohio-born Charles Francis Hall (centre) was among the most successful searchers, locating numerous artifacts and recording Inuit testimony through translators that continues to be cited today. Hall is shown here with his long-term Inuit companions and translators, Taqulittuk (left) and Ipiirvik (right), in an illustration from his book *Life with the Esquimaux*, published in 1865.

Even in summer, the weather in Beechey Island rarely breaks 10 degrees Celsius. On the island, where the expedition spent its first winter, the growing season lasts less than 60 days, and Arctic animals such as muskoxen are few. Had they not come well provisioned, it's unlikely Franklin's men would have survived a single winter.

ROB STIMPSON

MANY QUESTS FOR GLORY in the Arctic ended in some form of disaster, or dodged it by a miracle. While losing ships and some men was rather common, only one other expedition in history has vanished with no survivors. James Knight's 1719 voyage to discover the Northwest Passage ended in utter failure, with the loss of both ships and all forty sailors.[16]

Franklin's own first polar journey, an overland trek running from 1819 to 1822, was so sensational in its depraved details that it helped spark the subsequent decades of public fascination with the region. His published account became a Victorian and even an Edwardian bestseller, was reprinted three times in just eighteen months, was published in the United States, translated into French and German, and kept in print until the twentieth century.[17]

Viewed solely by its geographical achievements, Franklin's first Arctic trip was an extraordinary success, charting 340 kilometres of coastline. It added impetus to the British Admiralty's insistence on claiming the Northwest Passage and helped solidify the idea that it existed.[18]

It was a journey up and down rivers in heavily laden canoes and tramping over the tundra in the company of the famous voyageurs, with the intention of mapping the jagged interior coastline of North America's north-

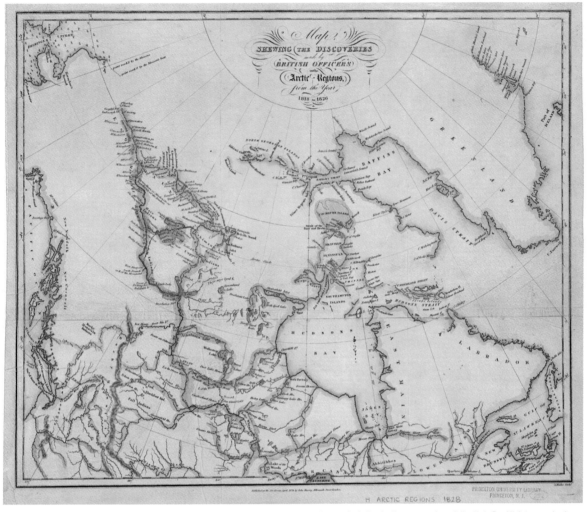

In 1828, Canada's central and western Arctic was mostly unknown to European cartographers, but much of what *had* been mapped owed directly to Franklin's two overland expeditions. Both expeditions mapped part of mainland North America, but the second was especially prolific. That expedition mapped over six hundred kilometres of coast to the west of the Coppermine River, visible in the top left of this map.

JOHN FRANKLIN, 1786–1847, "MAP SHEWING THE DISCOVERIES MADE BY THE BRITISH OFFICERS IN THE ARCTIC REGIONS, FROM THE YEARS 1818–1826."/J. WALKER SCULPT, LONDON: JOHN MURRAY, 1828/ HISTORIC MAPS COLLECTION, DEPARTMENT OF SPECIAL COLLECTIONS, PRINCETON UNIVERSITY LIBRARY

ern shore. At that time, little of that coast had been charted—and even less of the Arctic Archipelago. Every single kilometre had to be painstakingly, dangerously traversed and drawn, compass measurements taken at every turn. And those magnetic compass measurements were prone to error because the expedition was within range of the magnetic North Pole, and navigators were not yet able to properly calculate its effect on their readings.

It was perilous, exacting work, in aid of the most pressing political and scientific efforts of the day. And it was entrusted to the elite of British society, many of whom were also trained as scientists. Absent a war, it was one of the few ways an ambitious gentleman could achieve glory, riches and status. Franklin, like so many other polar explorers, was knighted for his efforts on behalf of the realm.

Franklin's 1819 overland expedition wrote his own future, in a sense. He established for the first time that it might be possible to sail from a certain point just above the North American coast all the way to the Pacific Ocean in the west. That idea opened up the possibility that one could sail through a route that Edward Parry had just recently discovered through Lancaster Sound, then south to the North American coast, and then all the way to the Pacific.[19] This is precisely the route Franklin was ordered to attempt in his final expedition in 1845.

Franklin's first overland expedition in 1819 was scientifically successful, but it was ill-planned and catastrophically ill-provisioned. This was partly the result of the haste with which it was put together and partly because the British Admiralty was relying on two private and warring fur companies, the Hudson's Bay Company and the North West Company, to help Franklin and his party find food. That failed.

Franklin nearly starved. But it wasn't just the lack of food that scotched the endeavour. The written records of the voyage show that Franklin pushed his men far past human limits in his urge to complete the mission he had been given. Even the voyageurs, famed for superior physical abilities on the demanding terrain, were pushed past exhaustion. Some were driven to death. Some starved. One appears to have murdered fellow voyageurs and eaten them and also to have killed one of Franklin's officers. That man was executed. All suffered from the decay of scurvy.

In the end, eleven of the twenty died—more than half—and the survivors were reduced to eating boiled lichen, old buffalo hides and every scrap of leather in sight. Franklin was ever after known as the man who ate his own boots. One account describes the men's rapture at finding plump insects in the rotting hides, juicy morsels to pop in their mouths before they ate the hides themselves. The remaining nine men were saved just days from death by starvation by the arrival of Yellowknife tribal hunters bearing fresh meat.

Franklin was rewarded with a second overland mission, which was not nearly as dramatic as the first. But it was also geographically important, helping to chart another 640 kilometres of the northern interior coast. Again, it helped spur the conviction among the Admiralty that a clear passage through the Arctic was tantalizingly within reach. By the time Franklin set out in 1845, just one hundred kilometres of the continent's mainland shoreline remained to be charted.[20]

But it was the fantastical events from the expedition in *Victory* commanded by John Ross in 1829 that may have most influenced the public view of Franklin's final journey. Ross and his nephew, James Clark Ross, got caught in the ice off Boothia Peninsula. After three winters, surviving in a camp by bartering with Inuit hunters and eating their fresh meat and fish to avoid scurvy, John Ross decided in the spring of 1832 to abandon his ship and march with his men several hundred kilometres north to Somerset Island on Lancaster Sound. But no ships arrived and they returned to their Somerset camp, though not the ship.

The following summer—it was now 1833—ill, starving, feeble and dressed in disintegrating animal skins, they again marched north, rowed for Baffin Island and waited. In August, they sighted two whaling ships, leapt into their boats, summoned their final reserves of energy, gave chase, rowing, and finally caught up to one of them.[21]

It was a miraculous rescue. Ross and his men had been considered dead for two years. In the end, only three of the twenty-two men were lost. The story again ignited Victorian imaginations. And it added fuel to several strong Victorian polar conceits: that man could, if he really wanted to, prevail over nature; that British know-how was globally infallible; and that one must never give up hope of rescue, even in one's darkest hour. The idea that it was blind luck, with some help from Inuit knowledge, and that luck might not strike again, was not commonly held.

Erebus and *Terror* had been modified to operate in polar conditions, but despite their reinforcements, the ships were not icebreakers. To make the most progress during the brief ice-free window of the polar summer, the men had to break ice by hand when they were able, as the crew of HMS *Terror* is shown doing here.

NATIONAL MARITIME MUSEUM, GREENWICH, LONDON

✦

As 1848 DAWNED, life on *Erebus* and *Terror* was disintegrating. Franklin was dead. Fitzjames had taken over as captain of *Erebus*. Crozier, captain of *Terror*, was now in command of the expedition. They were still prisoners of the ice, inching south along with it. The ice was stronger and more resilient than when it had first locked them in, and had built upon itself year after year. It had developed a life of its own. Massive, deadly chunks of ice thrust up against each other, rising high in the air. It would have been terrifying. And then, once summer came, the ice teased them. Perhaps beginning to melt, it gave them hope of release. But then it would muster again before they could get away, standing fast, thickening even when it ought to have been wasting away. How could the ice be so furious, so fat, so relentless? On board, the opposite was happening to the men. Scurvy and starvation were taking their toll, as was lead poisoning. They were getting thinner, weaker, more irresolute.

Lead poisoning has insidious effects on both body and mind. In the body, even tiny amounts can cause fatigue, digestive upset, headaches and joint pains. Lead is a potent neurotoxin, leading to memory loss, mood disorder, paranoia, pain, tingling and numbness in extremities and general mental breakdown. Could this have been a contributing factor in some of the decisions that were made? In a crisis, every decision is critical and requires clear thinking.

This may have been around the time that another puzzling, disturbing Inuit visit to a ship took place. It is not clear whether the visit, as told to Hall, was to one of Franklin's vessels, nor is it clear precisely when the visit took place, but the story is alarming. Told by Ookbarloo, it is the account of an Inuit hunter who came across a great ship stuck in the ice and was welcomed on board by the captain. He went to the ship again later, only to be captured and restrained by men whose faces, hands and clothing were black. The same captain he had seen before then came up to the deck and ordered the men to release him. They went back down into the bowels of the ship and the captain tried to reassure the Inuit hunter with a gift. At the same time, the captain pointed out a tent on the ice, saying that black-faced men lived there and warning the Inuit never to go near it.[22]

Woodman, who explored this story, wondered whether the men were covered in coal dust, because the steam engines on *Erebus* and *Terror* ran on coal. He also pointed out that the incident, if it referred to one of Franklin's ships, appeared to describe a ship bereft of naval discipline and possibly short of officers who could keep control. It is also possible that the men's scary faces were black as a result of advanced scurvy and that the episode happened after the initial abandonment of the ships. Another option Woodman suggested is that the men were celebrating Guy Fawkes Day.

Whatever else was happening, by early 1848, the deaths were mounting alarmingly, affecting officers far more than the other sailors. By April, according to additional information Franklin's men inserted into the margins of the jaunty first note left in the Victory Point cairn, 9 of the 21 officers were dead—or more than 40 per cent—as well as 15 of the 108 sailors—or about 14 per cent. This was a far greater rate of death than had afflicted most other Arctic expeditions. The Franklin disaster was already well advanced but had not yet reached its terrible end.

✦

IN BRITAIN, FRANKLIN'S WIFE, Lady Jane Franklin, a formidable and well-connected custodian of her husband's reputation, was starting to worry. More than two years had gone by since her husband set out. John Ross, who was an old friend of Franklin's, explained to the Admiralty that Franklin had privately asked him to send out a search party if he had not been heard from by the beginning of 1848.[23] By March, British parliamentarians started to talk of mounting relief expeditions. Within weeks, the rescue attempts began, as did the mounting obsession to figure out what had become of Franklin, his 128 men and *Erebus* and *Terror*.

It was a three-pronged effort: two ships to the eastern portion of the Northwest Passage through Lancaster Sound under the command of James Clark Ross; two to rendezvous at the western end via the Bering Strait and to traverse the passage from the west; and a third contingent down the Mackenzie River to the continent's northern shore, all on a mission to reach Franklin's men before it was too late.

When the Franklin expedition set sail, it was stocked with three years of supplies. Food canning was a cutting-edge food processing technology that allowed unprecedented preparation, but it hadn't been thoroughly tested. Lead solder sealing the cans seeped into the preserves, elevating levels of lead in the crew's bodies and likely leading to the death of some crew members.

Rope, belonging to Erebus and Terror, left at Beechy Island, 1847, and found Aug. 1850 by Capt. Austen.

Archaeologists are able to identify most Royal Navy property by the broad arrows it stamped on nearly every part of a ship to prevent theft. Rope could not be stamped, so coloured threads were integrated into its weave to identify a rope as Royal Navy property.

Spectacles with tinted lenses found in an abandoned boat at Erebus Bay, King William Island, in May 1859 by the McClintock Search Expedition 1857–59. The spectacles have straight, hinged sides and oval blue lenses; wire mesh remains on one side. They would have been intended to protect the wearer's eyes from snow blindness.

H. M. S.hips Erebus and Terror
{ Wintered in the Ice in
28 of May 1847 { Lat. 70°5' N Long. 98°23' W

Having wintered in 1846—7 at Beechey Island
in Lat 74°43'28" N. Long 91·39·15" W after having
ascended Wellington Channel to Lat 77°— and returned
by the West side of Cornwallis Island.

Sir John Franklin commanding the Expedition.
All well

Party consisting of 2 Officers and 6 Men
left the Ships on Monday 24th May 1847

Gm Gore Lieut
Chas F Des Vœux Mate

WHOEVER finds this paper is requested to forward it to the Secretary of
the Admiralty, London, with a note of the time and place at which it was
found: or, if more convenient, to deliver it for that purpose to the British
Consul at the nearest Port.

QUINCONQUE trouvera ce papier est prié d'y marquer le tems et lieu ou
il l'aura trouvé, et de le faire parvenir au plutot au Secretaire de l'Amirauté
Britannique à Londres.

CUALQUIERA que hallare este Papel, se le suplica de enviarlo al Secretario
del Almirantazgo, en Londrés, con una nota del tiempo y del lugar en
donde se halló.

EEN ieder die dit Papier mogt vinden, wordt hiermede verzogt, om het
zelve, ten spoedigste, te willen zenden aan den Heer Minister van de
Marine der Nederlanden in 's Gravenhage, of wel aan den Secretaris der
Britsche Admiraliteit, te London, en daar by te voegen eene Nota,
inhoudende de tyd en de plaats alwaar dit Papier is gevonden geworden.

FINDEREN af dette Papiir ombedes, naar Leilighed gives, at sende
samme til Admiralitets Secretairen i London, eller nærmeste Embedsmand
i Danmark, Norge, eller Sverrig. Tiden og Stædit hvor dette er fundet
önskes venskabeligt paategnet.

WER diesen Zettel findet, wird hier-durch ersucht denselben an den
Secretair des Admiralitets in London einzusenden, mit gefälliger angabe
an welchen ort und zu welcher zeit er gefunden worden ist.

London, John Murray, Albemarle Street 1859.

Despite much speculation, we know very little about the Franklin expedition's later days. This note—written originally by James Fitzjames in 1847, with margin notes added in 1848 by Fitzjames and Francis Crozier—was recovered from a stone cairn on King William Island by the McClintock Arctic Expedition in 1859. It tells us much of what we actually know. It is now part of the collection of the National Maritime Museum in Greenwich, London. Archaeological work on the wreck of *Erebus* promises to reveal answers Franklinophiles have sought for a century and a half.

Joseph Mathias Negelen/Wikimedia Commons

After the expedition's disappearance, Lady Jane Franklin funded search parties aiming to learn of her husband's fate, but she didn't sit at home wallowing in her loss. Lady Jane was a world traveller in her own right who had climbed Mount Olympus and sailed on the Nile. Even in her later years, she continued to travel abroad, taking her first trip to India at age 74.

THE 105 FRAIL, ADDLED MEN on *Erebus* and *Terror* knew nothing of these plans. It was Saturday, April 22, 1848, a portentous day of hope in the religious life of these men. Christianity was their unquestioned touchstone and this was the day after the crucifixion of Christ on Good Friday and before his resurrection on Easter Sunday. Was the Christian symbolism of the date an indication of their frame of mind? They were preparing to abandon ship under Crozier's direction. Rather than follow John Ross's example, the plan was to head south toward Back River (also known at that time as Great Fish River) on the mainland, where, with luck, they would manoeuvre by boat upriver to a trading station, Europeans, food and salvation. It would be a perilous journey of thousands of kilometres across the barren lands.

They modified some of the ships' boats for travel on a flowing river they could only imagine in this frozen landscape, and then lashed them to wooden sledges made on the ships. They filled the boats with tools, weapons and heavy equipment. And then they stacked in silks, scented soaps, an ivory-veneered wooden clothes brush, combs, slippers, silverware and toothbrushes. The expedition's copy of *The Vicar of Wakefield* was taken along and so was the Bible and some devotional reading. They brought tea and chocolate.[24] In all, each sledge would have weighed more than six hundred kilograms by the time they had finished, an enormous load to be hauled by desperately, multiply sick men, poorly equipped to withstand the horrors of the ice and remorseless cold.[25]

And then, on April 26, 1848, the startlingly large group abandoned the ships still locked in the ice. The men trudged across the frozen expanse, hauling sledges and boats by the strength of their shoulders and legs alone, dressed in English leather boots fitted with screws through their soles for grip, patterned cotton or silk neckerchiefs, blue wool uniforms and heavy blue woollen pilot-cloth overcoats that no longer fit—scrawny, stumbling figures headed south.[26]

The first Franklin expedition search parties set out when the expedition had not been heard from after three years. HMS *North Star* was sent in 1849 to resupply an early Royal Navy search party led by Sir James Clark Ross. This apparatus illustrates one of the methods used to clear ice, often in an attempt to free a ship.

RELICS BROUGHT BACK BY THE FRANKLIN SEA

Early search parties had no luck finding *Erebus*, *Terror* or any surviving crew, but did come across various relics the expedition left behind, including watches, guns and cutlery. This illustration appeared in *The Sea: Its Stirring Story of Adventure, Peril, and Heroism*, vol. 3, by Frederick Whymper, published in London in 1890.

PEDITION.

The Canadian flag snaps in the breeze over *One Ocean Voyager*.

JOHN GEIGER

CHAPTER 5

PRIDE

SEPTEMBER 8–10, 2014

OTTAWA AND GJOA HAVEN

IT WAS THE PHONE CALL that would mark the highlight of any cabinet minister's career. Leona Aglukkaq, member from Nunavut in Parliament and environment minister, was the first of the elected leaders to be informed of the find, according to protocol, and to her fell the privilege of informing the prime minister. She had been on the bridge of *Kingston* as Stephen Harper and the rest of the team had launched the season's search with a toast. Little had she known then that she would be making this call just a few weeks later. At ten in the morning on Monday, September 8, 2014, she phoned the prime minister at home.

He did a fist pump. A student of Franklin in his own right, he had been puzzling over the mystery of the ships' disappearance for years and had poured his own personal passion and his government's resources into solving it. And while it wasn't clear yet which of Franklin's ships had been discovered, he knew instantly that this was history in the making and perhaps even a new way for Canadians to understand themselves.

As Andrew Campbell, the government's executive in charge of the mission, put it, Canadians have a long history of building their narrative from the east to the west and occasionally to the south. But the moments when Canadians come together the most are when they direct that narrative—he calls it "pointing their toes"—to the north. To Jim Balsillie, it represented a beginning rather than an end, the chance for Canadians to explore how deeply the landscapes of the north have shaped the nation.

The next day, September 9, key members of the team came together again. The *Laurier* quickly headed back to Gjoa Haven where Marc-André Bernier, Ryan Harris, Jonathan Moore and Douglas Stenton caught flights to Ottawa. Geordie Dalglish, Andrew Prossin, André Préfontaine of the geo-

Prime Minister Stephen Harper (centre) announces the discovery of HMS *Erebus* with Parks Canada's Ryan Harris (left), Environment Minister Leona Aglukkaq (centre right), and John Geiger (right), CEO of The Royal Canadian Geographical Society, and Rear Admiral John Newton (far right). Tim MacDonald of the Arctic Research Foundation sits near left.

graphical society and Geiger had flown out of Cambridge Bay, as had Balsillie a little earlier. Balsillie and Tim MacDonald from the Arctic Research Foundation were there, as were John Newton and Aglukkaq. The small group sat at a table with the artifacts from the shore—clutched on the flights south by Stenton. Then the prime minister told the world about the find, revealing the haunting sonar images of the ship. Part of her skeleton was visible through the missing flesh of her deck, a gash out of her hull, with more of her timbers strewn on the sea floor. She was a shining form cradled by black shadows on a caramel-coloured background. To those involved in the search, the possibilities for solving further mysteries now seemed endless.

Harper, not given to extravagant displays of emotion, had a smile stretched broadly across his face. Later, Laureen Harper said that a friend had told her the prime minister looked "giddy," as she put it, drolly, "not a word one normally associates with my husband." But Harper knew it was a great moment in Canada's life, the sort of moment most countries experience only rarely.

"This is truly a historic moment for Canada," Harper said. "Franklin's ships are an important part of Canadian history given that his expeditions, which took place nearly two hundred years ago, laid the foundations of Canada's Arctic sovereignty. . . . Finding the first vessel will no doubt provide the momentum—or wind in our sails—necessary to locate its sister ship and find out even more about what happened to the Franklin expedition's crew."

Queen Elizabeth II, great-great-granddaughter of Queen Victoria, whose government sent Franklin on his expedition in 1845, issued a message of congratulation on the "historic achievement" through Governor General David Johnston.

The find instantly became an international phenomenon. The British Broadcasting Corporation quoted local Franklin scholar William Battersby saying it was "the biggest archaeological discovery the world has seen since the opening of Tutankhamun's tomb almost one hundred years ago."

The saga had immense resonance in the United Kingdom. The loss of the ships and the grisly tale of their doomed crew had been a British obsession for decades, abating only when it was replaced by the horrors and triumphs of the First World War. A key part of the international fascination was that Inuit knowledge had helped point the search in the right direction. It was as though two solitudes of the Victorian era—technologically advanced explorers and Inuit hunters—had finally, poetically, met in the present.

Meanwhile, Aglukkaq had left the press conference and was on her way to Gjoa Haven, the community on King William Island where she grew up, to tell the hamlet's elders about the find in their own language. On September 10, the whole community gathered to hear her and to meet the combined search team from *Laurier* and *Martin Bergmann*, both at anchor in the harbour. It was an emotional ceremony with a feast of caribou and Arctic char, followed by traditional drumming.

Environment Minister Leona Aglukkaq at the press conference announcing the discovery of *Erebus*.

Parks Canada's Ryan Harris and Prime Minister Stephen Harper announce the discovery of HMS *Erebus* at a press conference in Ottawa.

The discovery of *Erebus* hit close to home for Environment Minister and Nunavut MP Leona Aglukkaq, who is a native of Gjoa Haven and an Inuk.

Captain Bill Noon addresses the hamlet of Gjoa Haven, Nunavut. Scott Youngblut of the Canadian Hydrographic Service sits near left, while Louie Kamookak sits third from the left.

In his Captain's Log of September 16, 2014, Captain Bill Noon reflected on his experience at the gathering in Gjoa Haven: " One of the greatest honours for me took place on September 10 when I was invited to address the council in Gjoa Haven, along with the federal Minister of the Environment, the Honourable Leona Aglukkaq, the Premier of Nunavut, the Honourable Peter Taptuna, the Nunavut Minister of Finance, the Honourable Keith Peterson, and the mayor of Gjoa Haven, His Worship Allen Aglukkaq. Following that meeting, the hamlet held a community feast and put on a true northern celebration that included speeches, singing and drum dancing.

"As the celebration went on, I realized that this honour truly belongs to the Inuit. Over the years, I have read many accounts of the oral history, and I have been fortunate in being able to speak to many residents of Gjoa Haven. In particular much credit goes to Louie Kamookak, a local well-respected Franklin historian. The Inuit stories held true.

"Since this project began in earnest in 2008 (when making our own charts was needed simply to get into this area), the specialized knowledge, talents and skills of those aboard have been shared freely. In hindsight, this resulted in a scenario where pilots became archeologists; hydrographers became historians; professional mariners became hydrographers; archeologists and ship captains became diplomats; and all aboard became aware of the significant value of Inuit traditional knowledge."

Tyrone Burke/*Canadian Geographic*

Historically, Inuit drumming was exclusively the domain of Inuit men. Young men like Peter Jayko in Gjoa Haven have kept the tradition alive, but now some young girls and women in the community also choose to learn drumming.

Like many others intimately involved with the search, Louie Kamookak was so overcome that he began to weep. "We are all working together to put the puzzle pieces in their right places," says Kamookak of the search. "It is because of this co-operation that our dream is finally being realized." To Kamookak, a teacher at Qiqirtaq Ilihakvik High School in Gjoa Haven, the Franklin story was far more than a personal passion. It was about the value of his traditions and culture, about the land where he grew up, where he lives still, where he continues to hunt and fish, and where his elders first told him their stories of the doomed expedition. "I think that there will be more interest in [Inuit traditional knowledge] now, and not only in the south. Even for a lot of younger people in the North it's kind of a new thing coming out that the Franklin ship is found."

Standing there at the ceremony, with the tears flowing, he thought of all the elders who had carried the tales so faithfully for so long and yet had not lived to hear of the find, he said. "But it was only through the hard work of the people at Parks Canada that it was made possible." Ever since the Canadian government plucked him from his ancestral hunting grounds at the age of nine and enrolled him in the school newly built on the island, Kamookak has been captivated by the tale of the men who could not survive in his people's land. "From day one I have been curious about what happened to those ships," he says. He had heard a version of it from his own relatives, passed down by oral story for all those generations. But at school, for the first time he heard the European versions, as well as European interpretations of the accounts from Inuit. Those accounts have more often than not been considered wildly unreliable by non-Inuit. For example, a famous map made in 1927 by the British Admiralty's cartographer Rupert Thomas Gould, with notations about all the Franklin findings to that date, labels Inuit testimony "altogether not trustworthy."[27]

Kamookak's lifelong quest had been to discern the truth by sifting through the different stories and comparing them. He dreams even now about finding Franklin's grave, fondly replaying in his imagination the scene reuniting Sir John in death with his wife, Lady Franklin, in London. "If he was found," says Kamookak of Franklin, "then Lady Jane Franklin's wishes that she have a place next to her husband could be fulfilled. I know the feeling that she had. If my wife was gone, I would want her to come back to me. The same is true of anyone I love. It's true of my daughters, of my granddaughter. I would want to be with them." He has scoured his island and many of the others in this part of the Arctic Archipelago for decades, finding artifacts that might have been related to the expedition, often leaving them on the ground for future archaeological investigation.

He is so tied to the story that on April 22, 1998, for the 150th anniversary, he and a friend were commissioned by the community of Gjoa Haven to erect a plaque on King William Island to memorialize the spot where Franklin's surviving 105 men abandoned their ships to the ice, casting their fate to the frozen land.

Perhaps more importantly, Kamookak and his wife, Josephine—the last young couple in Gjoa Haven to have had an arranged marriage—have spent years putting together maps of traditional place names in that part of the Arctic. Inuit names are embedded with information that a satellite-based GPS reading, though geographically precise, cannot contain: what kind of landscape it is, its potential dangers, what could be hunted there, how it fit into Inuit culture. Knowing all that traditional information helped Kamookak

Drumming is a part of traditional Inuit celebrations, and when *Erebus* was found drummers of all ages, including Jacob Atqittuk, came together in Gjoa Haven to perform for the community and searchers.

unravel the meaning contained in some of the Victorian Franklin accounts, and that, in turn, helped him figure out where Franklin's ship might have ended up.

By 2006, when Parks Canada and Robert Grenier, then chief of Underwater Archaeology, again began plans to search for Franklin—searches started two years later—Kamookak's expertise, the entire body of Inuit traditional knowledge about a wreck in the eastern Queen Maud Gulf and the work of past searchers influenced the focus of the search in this wide area, a place where Aglukkaq was now telling their people the ship had been found.

And then, as with so many Inuit ceremonies, the feast began. The people of Gjoa Haven, some perhaps descendants of those who walked these lands when Franklin's men marched to their death, were relishing the food from their own land, singing the songs of their ancestors, dancing the traditional steps, listening to the ancient beat of the drum. Underpinning it all was the confirmation that their elders had been telling the truth and that they had also passed it down faithfully through all those generations. It was nothing short of a vindication of the Inuit culture.

The remarkable find was a cause for celebration and pride; however, it was also imbued with a certain poignancy. *Erebus* was a stark reminder that many of the 129 men had died horrific deaths. From those first images captured by Parks Canada divers, you could see enough of the ship, with her remarkable craftsmanship, imbued with Victorian culture, perverted from her great purpose and now disabled on the ocean floor. There was a sense of loss mixed in with the victory and the celebration. As long as mystery prevailed, so did the possibilities. Now it was clear where the Franklin story ended.

Inuit oral history expert Louie Kamookak speaks at a community gathering in Gjoa Haven, Nunavut, shortly after *Erebus* was found.

Tyrone Burke/Canadian Geographic

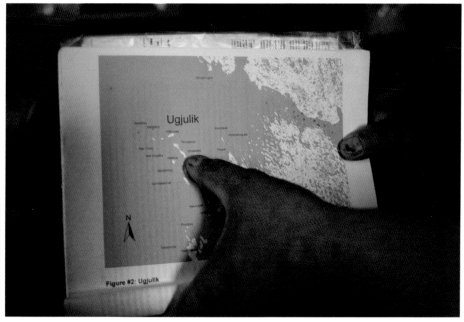

Inuit testimony placed the ship near the Adelaide Peninsula in Queen Maud Gulf, near where it was ultimately found.

Inuit testimony has proven accurate, but it is not always precise, as stories of different explorers can blend together. To best understand the past, Inuit testimony expert Louie Kamookak—shown here in his cabin near Gjoa Haven holding an original copy of Charles Francis Hall's writings—cross-references Inuit accounts with the journals of European and North American explorers.

A detail from a chromoxylograph featuring *Erebus* and *Terror* among icebergs, from the book *The Polar World* by G. Hartwig, published 1874, London.

CHAPTER 6

MARCH OF DEATH

THEY MUST HAVE KNOWN it was a bold strategy—perhaps a mad one—setting off across the blinding, frozen stretch of Arctic land, lugging their possessions behind them on cumbersome sledges. They would certainly have known that they were sick and that too many of their comrades—twenty-four, including Franklin—had already succumbed to illness. But who among the ailing 105 men could imagine the horrors to which some of them would stoop in the months to come as they struggled to survive?

They were under the command of Francis Crozier, captain of *Terror*, who had taken over the expedition command following Franklin's death. Second-in-command was James Fitzjames, the promising young leader who had written such amusing portraits of his crewmates and sent them back to Britain just before his ship, *Erebus*, entered the Northwest Passage in August 1845. They were headed south on foot, dragging their supplies toward the mouth of Back River on the mainland of the continent. Perhaps they were aiming for the fertile hunting grounds of the mainland, hoping to shoot caribou and wildfowl and restore themselves to health. If they had been able to do that and then to follow the river's arduous ascent hundreds of kilometres by boat, they would have eventually reached a Hudson's Bay Company post, Fort Resolution, on the south side of Great Slave Lake.

Or, as they shambled away from the ships, would the men have understood the hopelessness of their situation? Did they know they were marching to their death? Were Crozier and Fitzjames able to shore up their spirits? Did they convince the men they could make it back to Britain alive, that they could withstand the ice?

Taken from John Franklin's *Narrative of a Journey to the Shores of the Polar Sea in the Years 1819-20-21-22*, this illustration shows Franklin's party crossing a frozen Great Slave Lake, Northwest Territories.

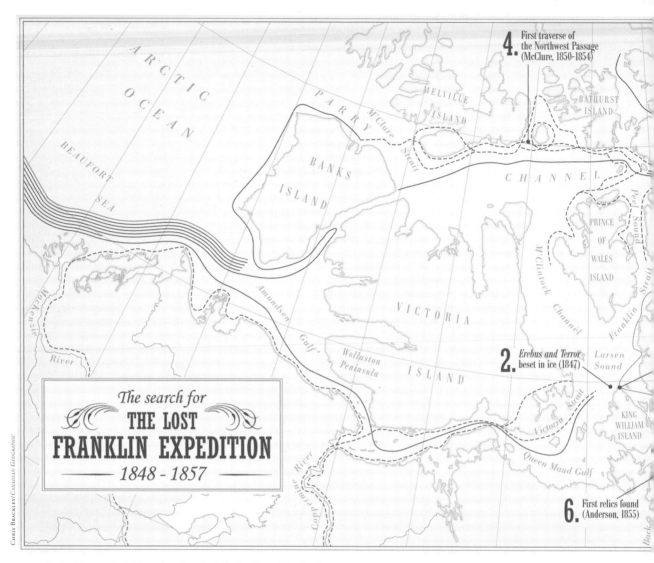

The search for THE LOST FRANKLIN EXPEDITION 1848 - 1857

CHRIS BRACKLEY/*CANADIAN GEOGRAPHIC*

4. First traverse of the Northwest Passage (McClure, 1850-1854)

2. *Erebus and Terror* beset in ice (1847)

6. First relics found (Anderson, 1855)

The Royal Navy was the first to send search parties for the Franklin expedition, but they came up empty-handed, and the Admiralty offered £20,000—a fortune at the time—for information about its ships or their crews. Dozens more search parties followed, culminating in the discovery of *Erebus* more than a century and a half later.

WHILE FRANKLIN'S MEN were on the march, the Admiralty sent out three expeditions to find them, the first of what would be thirty-six search, relief, rescue and recovery missions by 1859,[28] sent by many nations and individuals. The Admiralty did not know where Franklin could have been stuck, or even his precise route, so they sent one rescue party into the Northwest Passage from the west through the Bering

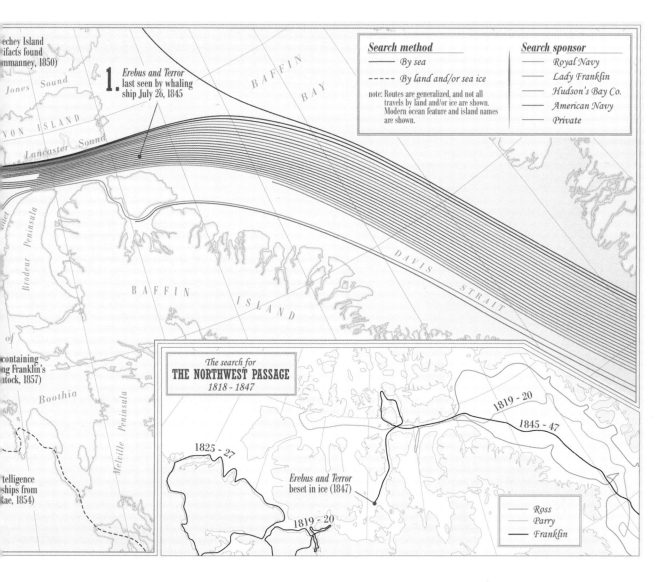

Sea. Another came down the mighty Mackenzie River to the north shore of the continent, well to the west of the Arctic Archipelago. The hope was to intercept Franklin, his men and their two ships, perhaps just above the westernmost part of the continent en route to the Pacific Ocean. The assumption was that they would have jubilantly completed the Northwest Passage or would have been caught somewhere just above the continent's northern edge.

James Clark Ross, the nephew of Franklin's great friend John Ross, had a more complicated remit. He was to take two ships in the general direction of King William Island, retracing Franklin's supposed route as much as possible, armed with ice sledges. He had enough food for three years, much of it tinned, along with extra provisions for Franklin's men should they be found. Within five months after Franklin's men abandoned their ships, and likely while some were still alive, he reached Somerset Island in the great whaling

M'Clintock's travelling party discovering the remains of Cairn at Cape Herschel

The McClintock Arctic Expedition is shown here travelling King William Island by sledge in the late 1850s.

THE VOYAGE OF THE FOX: A NARRATIVE OF THE DISCOVERY OF THE FATE OF SIR JOHN FRANKLIN, 1860, CAPT. F.L. McCLINTOCK/NATIONAL OCEANIC AND ATMOSPHERIC ADMINISTRATION/DEPARTMENT OF COMMERCE

route of Lancaster Sound. It was a natural rendezvous for a rescue expedition from Britain and it was, significantly, where Ross and his uncle spent time in the 1830s after having been forced to abandon their ship *Victory*. It was from this island that they launched the famous feats that ended with their own miraculous return to England after four winters in the ice.

But in the summer of 1848, Franklin's men were not there. They had not come this way—it was to the north and a little east of where *Erebus* and *Terror* were beset in the ice—but instead were marching south to Back River. They were moving away from the expedition that had the best chance of rescuing them.

Both the climate and the topography of King William Island were against the men. In the words of one of Franklin's subsequent searchers, Francis Leopold McClintock, the insalubrious air was filled with "chilling fogs," beset with cold northwest winds; "nothing can exceed the gloom and desolation of the western coast of King William Island."[29]

Franklin's men were traversing one of the grimmest parts of the Arctic. It had a low coast—McClintock described it as limestone shingle—and was considered inhospitable even by the Inuit, who tended to shun it. Inuit hunted only seal and sometimes polar bear in this part of the Arctic, because the usual prey, such as muskox, were uncommon and the polar bear population low. There was hardly enough game to feed small, roving Inuit hunting parties, and some Inuit had died of starvation on the island. It was folly to believe that the island could produce enough game to save this starving group of 105 men.

The search party led by Francis Leopold McClintock created this map in 1859, noting the locations where Franklin expedition relics had been found on King William Island.

Inuit went to this part of the island sporadically to hunt. Nevertheless, some of Franklin's wandering men came across a small group of perhaps four families of Inuit hunters after they began their final journey. That part is known because would-be rescuers and diagnosticians of Franklin's fate, including John Rae, McClintock, Charles Francis Hall and the American explorer Frederick Schwatka and his men, interviewed those same Inuit in the years and decades that followed, using their own local language skills and interpreters. In addition to direct discussions with Europeans and Americans, Inuit also passed down their knowledge of what happened to Franklin's men orally within their own communities. And while there are some inconsistencies among the accounts, a poignant vignette has emerged of what Franklin's remaining men faced on the land.

They had trekked all the way to the island's southern coast, to Washington Bay, by the time they met the Inuit, the only other humans they would encounter before their lives ended. The number of Franklin's men with the party at this point is unclear. Possibly some or even most had already died. Some may have broken away from the main group to fend for themselves or return to the ship, an indicator that discipline had broken down badly. But these men were able to indicate to the Inuit hunters by sign language that they

Search parties for Franklin used sledges in their overland searches for signs of the Franklin expedition, though this image is more fanciful than accurate. In 1879, Frederick Schwatka's expedition located human remains, giving them a simple burial.

were hungry and mimed the actions of catching a seal by cutting a hole in the ice to show the Inuit what they wanted. The Inuit gave the leader a small piece of seal meat and the leader asked that every Inuit pack be opened and examined for the presence of meat. He took some from each hunter, piled it on the back of an Inuit dog and had it taken to his men nearby, paying for it with a knife.

Franklin's men were putting up tents. They looked sick. One man's eyes were sunken. Some of the men had mouths that were hard and black, with gums so swollen they covered the teeth—signs of advanced scurvy. Some of them were very thin. It was clear that their bodies were shattered and perhaps their spirits too. Their science had failed them and so had their technology. All the Victorian culture they had so confidently brought with them from Britain was not able to save them. They didn't know how to keep themselves alive.

The Inuit left them the next morning, likely knowing that they had no way of helping the British men stave off starvation. The leader tried to stop them, seeming to say the Inuit word for "seal." But the hunters pressed on, leaving the Europeans behind.

Ross, meanwhile, had spent his only winter in the ice near Somerset Island and, by spring, was exploring its frozen western shoreline by sledge. He was moving over land in the direction Franklin took, but was forced to turn back before he got very far south. Illness was rampant on his expedition, and he had suffered twice as many deaths among his men as even Franklin had in his first year away, 1845 to 1846. Rather than risk more of his men's lives, and certain that Franklin was already on his way back to England, he decided to sail home.[30]

"I cannot help fearing that had we remained out an other winter, few if any would ever have returned," wrote the expedition's surgeon, John Robertson.[31] By November 1849, Ross was back in England. The other two rescue missions failed as well.

Ross's ships, HMS *Enterprise* and HMS *Investigator*, were swiftly outfitted anew and sent back to the polar regions under the command of Richard Collinson. Collinson was instructed to travel south around South America, up the west side of the Americas and into the passage from the west. The ships would become separated in the Pacific, and *Investigator,* under Robert McClure, would eventually be caught in the ice in Mercy Bay just off the coast of Banks Island and would be abandoned. Her crew would be saved. The sunken ship would be discovered in 2010 right where she was known to have sunk by the same Parks Canada underwater archaeologists who found *Erebus.*

But it was not only the British government that sent out expeditions to find Franklin. A patchwork of vessels funded publicly and privately, joined the quest, a feat of partnership echoed more than a century and a half later in the Canadian search for *Erebus.* John Ross, Franklin's friend, had harnessed the growing public fixation with Franklin to raise money by subscription for a yacht to join the search. The tireless Lady Franklin, meanwhile, outfitted her own ship—the first of several—and called for a national day of prayer for her husband.

Not content with raising support at home, she also wrote to Nicholas I, the Russian czar, pleading with him to search for her missing husband along the Bering Strait and the coast of Siberia.[32] As well, she appealed to U.S. president Zachary Taylor, asking for help and reminding him that Americans might finally claim the prize of completing the vaunted Northwest Passage as they sought her husband. The American government was not initially eager to assist but, prompted by the American philanthropist Henry Grinnell, eventually agreed to provide officers for two ships on Grinnell's promise he would fund the expedition. A keen tactician, Lady Franklin was anxious to keep up the pressure on the British government to continue the search, so she informed British officials that Americans were on the hunt for the passage as well as the missing ships.[33]

The Northwest Passage was crawling with rescue missions. The obsession to find the passage had been replaced with the obsession to find Franklin.

THE INUIT DID NOT HAVE further contact with survivors of Franklin's expedition, but they eventually saw the heartbreaking evidence of the Europeans' fate: corpses. They took belongings from their bags and sledges, some of which they traded back to the Europeans who came looking for Franklin. The books and records that they found, however—so painstakingly written and valuable to those who wished to understand what happened to the expedition—they gave to their children as playthings. Most revealing of all, perhaps, is that the Inuit took note of where they had seen all the human remains and were able to inform the later searchers of their location with pinpoint precision. These searchers then investigated the sites for themselves.

The picture that emerged was unspeakably grisly. Down the western coast of King William Island, within 130 kilometres of where they abandoned the ships, disease apparently overtook Franklin's men. Modern examination of the bones showed signs of advanced scurvy with its characteristic hemorrhaging on the bone.[34] The men were forced to stop marching and, in a place later called Terror Bay, they set up what looked to be a field hospital on top of a sandy hill. Three men died and were buried carefully there. By early June, when the wildfowl migrated north, the men shot the birds in robust numbers, leaving bones picked clean.

But by the time the Inuit found the tent site—possibly the following spring, although David Woodman put it a couple of years later—no one was left alive. Instead, they found the wildfowl bones plus numerous frozen human bodies, some in tents, some under a boat, some scattered along the shoreline. The bones of some of the bodies were skilfully butchered for meat, skulls broken open for their high-calorie brains.[35] Inuit also reported finding tall boots partially filled with boiled human flesh.

Some marchers eventually made their way to the mainland, toward Back River, likely carrying their comrades' heads, arms, hands and legs—sawn off and made portable—as a ready supply of calories.[36] The depravation came to naught. Another group of the men died at a spot later named Starvation Cove, along the way to the river.

DESPITE ALL THE SEARCHES, the Victorians knew nothing of what Franklin's men endured until John Rae, a talented overland explorer with the Hudson's Bay Company, sent word back to Britain in October 1854. Rae had helped to lead the overland expedition commissioned in 1848 as part of the first trio of Admiralty searches and had conducted two additional land searches for Franklin. But in 1854, he was attempting to complete the mapping of the Northwest Passage and by chance came upon some Inuit who told him of a

MAP

of the Sledge Journeys and Searches
of the Franklin Search Party under
LIEUT. FRED'K SCHWATKA,
1878-79-80.

Sledge Journey to King William Land and, return ·······▶·······
Preliminary Sledge Journeys of Lt. Schwatka
Col. Gilder

Taking on Inuit eating habits allowed Frederick Schwatka to tackle the 5,202-kilometre overland trek illustrated here. At the time, it was the longest sledge trek undertaken by a polar explorer. On the gruelling journey, Schwatka's team found parts of the ships' boats, buttons and graves, but concluded that no scientific record of the expedition existed. The notation "Ship Sank" (upper left) is very close to where the wreck of *Erebus* was found.

"Map of the sledge journeys and searches . . . in the search for Franklin: A narrative of the American expedition under Lieutenant Schwatka." G665 1878 S4 1888/Rom2014_14276_1/ROM Images

Painted for the 50th anniversary of the Franklin expedition, W. Thomas Smith's *They Forged the Last Link with Their Lives: HMS* Erebus *and* Terror, *1849–50* works from the premise that Franklin and his men were the first to discover a route through the uncharted Northwest Passage, based on the findings of the McClintock Arctic Expedition.

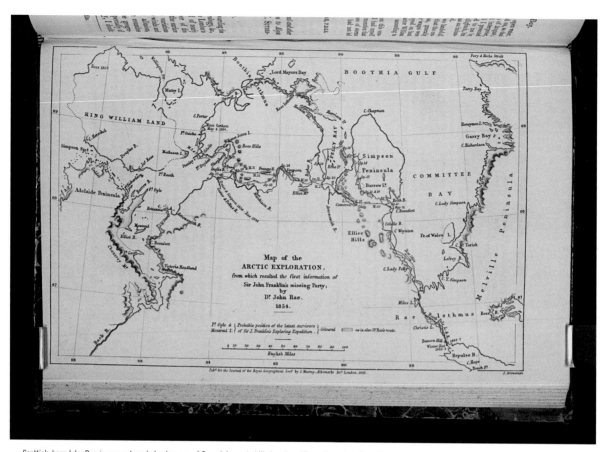

Scottish-born John Rae is now acknowledged as one of Canada's most skilled and prolific northern travellers, but when his 1854 search for the Franklin expedition (route shown here) turned up accounts of cannibalism in the Royal Navy, Rae was denounced as a liar by many in the United Kingdom.

party of Europeans who had pulled sledges down the west side of King William Island, that many had died of starvation near the mouth of Back River and that some had eaten each other to stave off death. They told of no survivors.

The Inuit showed Rae artifacts that they had removed from some of the sites where the men had fallen, and Rae traded goods to get them back. However, he failed to travel to the spot where the Inuit said some of the men's corpses were, because it was too late in the season, and headed back to Britain. He took the artifacts to London, including Franklin's gold Hanoverian Order of Merit, a silver-plated dessert spoon in a fiddle pattern featuring Franklin's crest, buttons and a gold cap band. That these possessions were in Inuit hands was taken to mean that something dire had happened to the expedition. And then, of course, there were the tales of corpses, starvation and cannibalism.

On August 4, 1854, Rae reported his findings to Sir George Simpson, governor of the Hudson's Bay Company, in a letter subsequently published in a newspaper: "From the mutilated state of many of the

National Maritime Museum, Greenwich, London

With numerous expeditions visiting the Arctic and the Inuit's ingenuity in turning items left behind into tools that were sometimes carried great distances, the provenance of artifacts is not always certain. This watch, likely manufactured in London between 1839 and 1857, is thought to be a relic of the Franklin expedition, but this is not certain.

National Maritime Museum, Greenwich, London

When possible, the Inuit made use of materials that explorers left behind. The knife shown here on the left was fashioned from Franklin expedition relics. The expedition led by Francis Leopold McClintock purchased it in 1859.

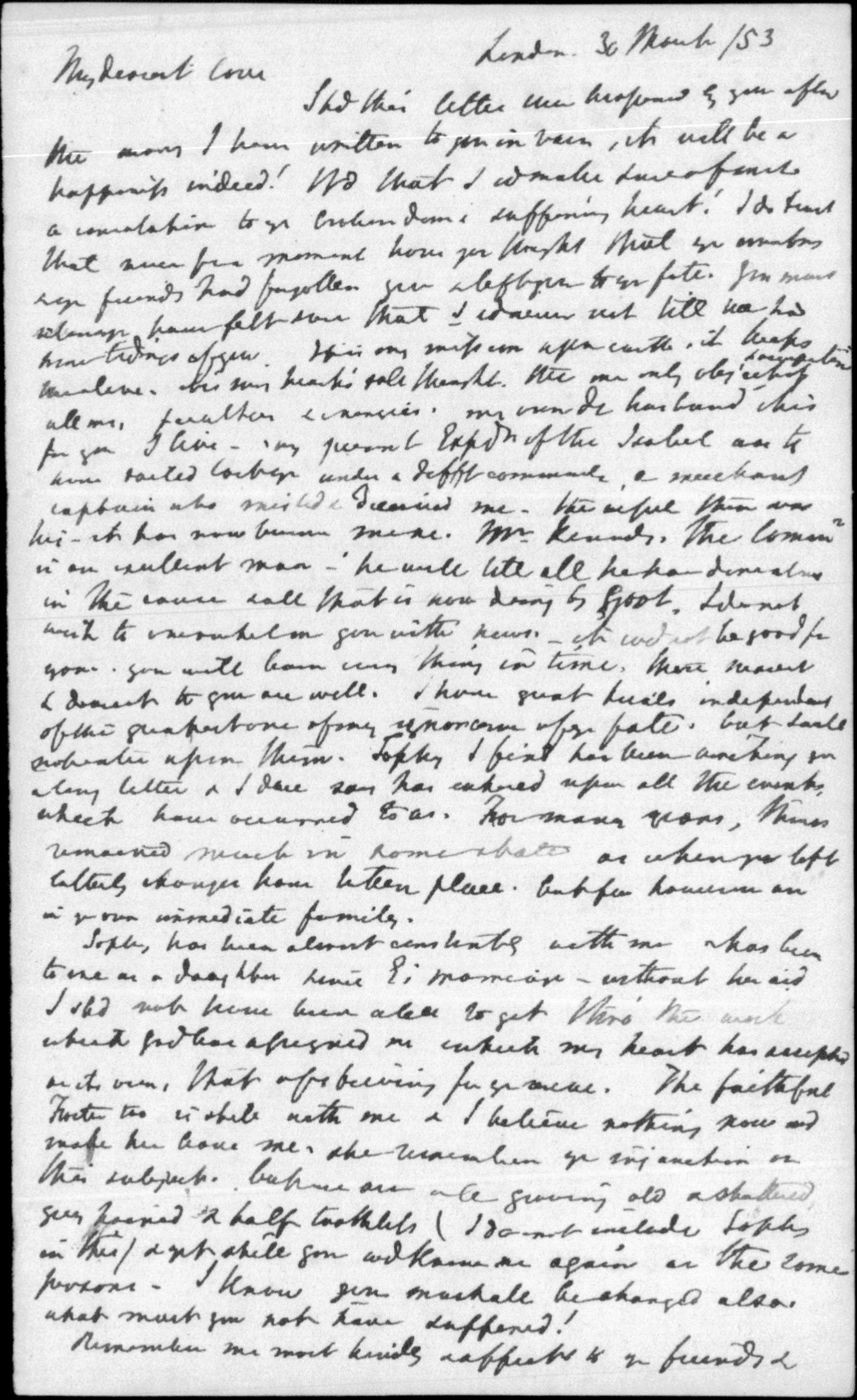
London. 30 March /53

My dearest Love

Shd this letter be [illegible] by you after the many I have written to you in vain, it will be a happiness indeed! Oh that I cd make sure of its being a consolation to yr broken down & suffering heart! I do trust that never for a moment have you thought that yr country & yr friends had forgotten you & left you to yr fate. You must always have felt sure that I cd never rest till we had some tidings of you. This is my mission upon earth. It keeps me alive. It is my heart's sole thought. The one only object [illegible] all my faculties & energies. My own dear husband [illegible] for you I live — my present Expdn of the Isabel was to have sailed long ago under a diffnt command, a merchant captain who misled & deceived me. The vessel then was his — it has now become mine. Mr. Kennedy, the Commr is an excellent man — he will tell all he has done also in the course & all that is now doing by Govt. I do not wish to overwhelm you with news — it wd not be good for you. You will learn every thing in time. Those nearest & dearest to you are well. I have great trials independently of the great one of my ignorance of yr fate, but I will not dwell upon them. Sophy I find has been writing you a long letter & I dare say has entered upon all the events which have occurred to us. For many years, things remained much in the same state as when you left, latterly changes have taken place. But few however are in yr own immediate family.

Sophy has been almost constantly with me & has been to me as a daughter since E's marriage — without her aid I shd not have been able to get thro' the work which God has assigned me & which my heart has accepted as its own, that of [illegible] for yr rescue. The faithful Foster too is still with me & I believe nothing now wd make her leave me. She remembers yr injunction on this subject. But we are all growing old & shattered, grey haired & half toothless (I do not include Sophy in this) & yet while you wd know us again as the same persons — I know you must all be changed also. What must you not have suffered!

Remember me most kindly & affectly to yr friends &

Lady Jane Franklin penned this letter to her husband in March 1853. He had been dead for more than six years at the time and she had not seen him since his final expedition set sail in May 1845.

corpses, and the contents of the kettles, it is evident that our miserable countrymen had been driven to the last resource—cannibalism—as a means of prolonging life."[37]

Victorian Britain was outraged. It was fresh from the triumph of the Great Exhibition of 1851, a celebration of modern industry and technology, a public show of British superiority, of hope in a bright future. Queen Victoria's consort, Prince Albert, had helped to bring the self-financing exhibition to a successful finish. Its substantial financial surplus was underwriting the construction of a spate of new cultural institutions along Exhibition Road in London's South Kensington. The idea that some of the esteemed Empire's naval men—symbols in their own right of Britain's technological might and sophistication—could have broken the taboo of cannibalism was simply unacceptable. It even displaced news of the quickly unfolding Crimean War.

Many observers refuted the claims or decided that the Inuit were the cannibals. The journalist and novelist Charles Dickens was encouraged by Lady Franklin to write a two-part story in his publication *Household Words*, dismissing the claims as "the chatter of a gross handful of uncivilised people, with a domesticity of blood and blubber."[38]

Finally, Lady Franklin procured enough money and support to launch yet another search party. She bought the steam yacht *Fox* and hired the vastly experienced Royal Navy captain Francis Leopold McClintock, who had taken part in three earlier searches for Franklin, including the first one to Somerset Island with James Clark Ross. The expedition set out in the middle of 1857.

✦

MCCLINTOCK SWIFTLY GOT CAUGHT in the ice, like most other polar explorers. But by April 1859, he at last made progress. He and his second-in-command, William Hobson, travelled to King William Island by sledge. McClintock took the east and south coasts, while Hobson searched the north and west. Quickly McClintock met Inuit who told him some of the same stories they had told Rae and allowed him to barter for silver utensils they had collected. The silver pieces were from Franklin and others of his expedition. The Inuit spoke of Europeans who dropped dead as they walked, of a group of Europeans who tried to get to a large river, hauling boats, and they said that Inuit had seen two big ships. They had boarded one ship and found a body, and they saw one ship that had sunk.

McClintock found a few relics on an island at the mouth of Back River and then headed toward King William Island's snowy southern shore, conscious of the fact that he was likely walking in the steps of Franklin's men. Just after midnight on May 24, 1859, he came across his first corpse, dressed in the uniform of a naval steward, a manservant of one of the ships' officers, some of his bones and clothing sticking out above the snow. Several clues about what he and the other men must have experienced were evident.[39]

For one thing, he appeared to have walked until he died, or fallen asleep as he stood and then perished, pushed to the absolute limits of his strength. If he was with shipmates, why did no one pick him up or bury him? Were

Franklin searchers mapped much of Canada's Arctic, and their ability to do this was bolstered by Francis Leopold McClintock's innovations to sledging, which dramatically extended maritime expeditions' ability to travel overland. McClintock's sledge system involved teams of six or seven men instead of dogs, sledge sails, advance parties that laid down food, and a support party during the early stages of a journey.

The Voyage of the 'Fox' in the Arctic Seas: A Narrative of the Discovery of the Fate of Sir John Franklin and His Companions, Capt. F.L. McClintock (1819–1907), London, 1859/Wikimedia Commons

they too exhausted themselves, or indifferent? If he was alone, why was he alone? In addition, he was dressed in absurdly inappropriate clothing for an overland march in the Arctic: a blue woollen jacket with slashed sleeves decorated with braid, a neckerchief loosely tied in a bow knot and a blue woollen pilot-cloth greatcoat.

McClintock also found a notebook, frozen shut. But once thawed, it proved to contain mysterious messages written in an unknown hand, some with words written backwards and ending in capital letters. Some were indecipherable gibberish. One contained the childlike drawing of an eye overtop the words "lid bay," while another featured words written in a circle around the phrase "the terror camp clear."[40]

Six days later, on the treacherous west coast, McClintock came across a boat found earlier by Hobson that had been modified and mounted onto an ice sledge, which he concluded likely came from *Erebus* because its pemmican tin was marked with an *E* and many of the items belonged to men from that ship. It contained the skeletons of two of Franklin's men, each missing his head.[41] His great surprise, however, was that the boat was facing north, toward the site where Franklin's men had abandoned their ships. This raised intriguing questions for McClintock and for Hobson, whose team had dug the boat out of deep snow.[42] Were the men returning to the ships? Did some of their shipmates leave them here, return to the ships themselves and intend to come back to rescue the men? Was the position insignificant, just an accident or a means for the men to shelter themselves from the howling Arctic wind?

Another puzzle was the contents of the boat. The well-worn copy of *The Vicar of Wakefield* was there along with a heavily underlined copy of the Bible. In addition, there was a "quantity of articles of one description and another truly astonishing in variety, and such as, for the most part, modern sledge-travelers in these regions would consider a mere accumulation of dead weight, but slightly useful and very likely to break down the strength of the sledge-crews."[43] In addition to the weighty material, there was the frippery of the Victorian age: silk handkerchiefs, seven or eight pairs of boots of different types, and calfskin-lined slippers edged in red silk ribbon.

With allegations of cannibalism shocking Victorian Britain, Lady Jane Franklin funded an 1857 expedition to explore her husband's mysterious fate. Captained by Francis Leopold McClintock, this mission aboard the steam yacht *Fox*, pictured here, found no surviving crewmen, but did yield the note in a cairn on Victory Point, which survives as the only written record of the Franklin expedition's later days.

It was Hobson who had made the grandest discovery, however. He and his team found the only official record of the expedition written by Franklin's officers. It had been left at the Victory Point cairn on land adjacent to where the men abandoned their ships. The record, as originally written in 1847, told about the success of the mission's first year, saying that all was well. Then, written in the margins of the same document the following year, was the chronicle of Franklin's death, of the deaths of twenty-three others, and of the desertion of the ships and the plan to get to Back River. Finally, here was the expedition's own partial account of what had happened and the plan of how the remaining men intended to get back home.

Once McClintock's findings became known in Britain, Franklin's reputation underwent a reformation. He was dead long before the cannibalism began and so could not be directly implicated. Even John Delane, the influential editor of *The Times*, who had frequently been a critic of the unending and expensive searches for Franklin, referred to the dead explorer as a King Arthur figure, recreating the Northwest Passage and the frozen Arctic as a modern Tintagel complete with heroic knights.[44]

THE AMERICAN FRANKLIN SEARCH EXPEDITION : CROSSING SIMPSON'S STRA
FROM A SKETCH BY MR. H. W. KLUTSCHAK.

Seen here crossing the Simpson Strait on a flotilla of kayaks, an American Geographical Society expedition led by Lieutenant Frederick Schwatka in 1878–80 was one of many sent to seek signs of Franklin and his men.

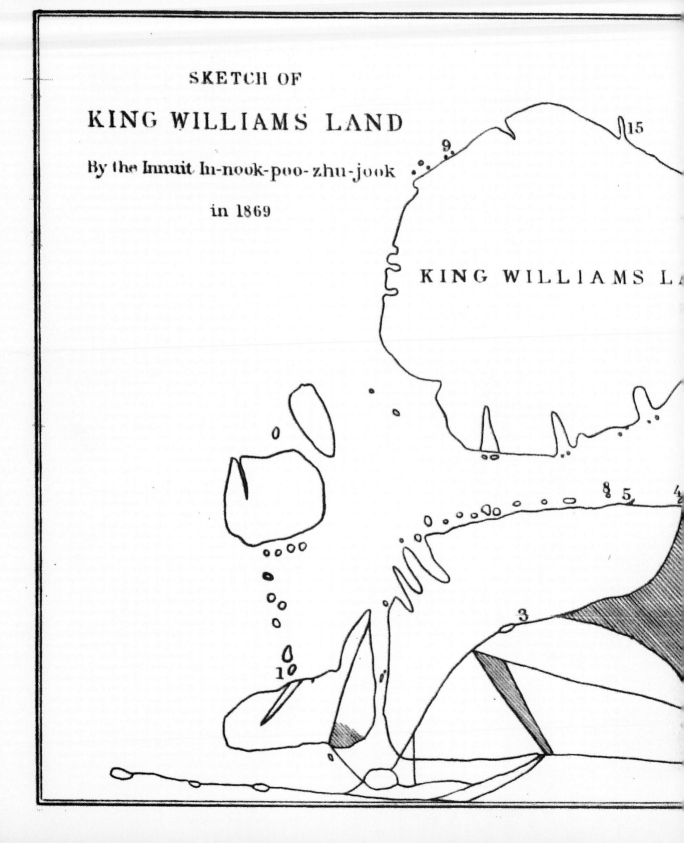

SKETCH OF

KING WILLIAMS LAND

By the Innuit In-nook-poo-zhu-jook

in 1869

KING WILLIAMS LA

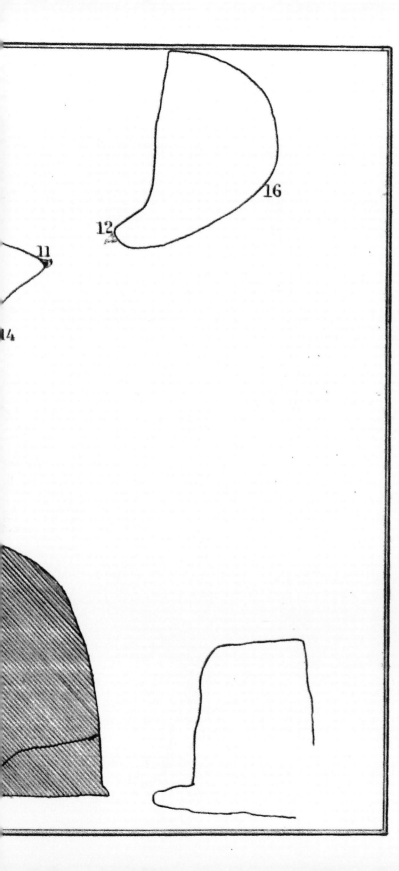

This map drawn by an Inuk named In-nook-poo-zhu-jook was reproduced in Hall's account of his second Arctic expedition. The number "1" in the bottom left denotes the location of the wreck of one of Franklin's ships in Ookgoolik, according to In-nook-poo-zhu-jook.

SOME INUIT ACCOUNTS CONTINUED to be riddles, however. Kokleearngnun told of witnessing a ship crushed by ice as men worked to remove provisions and put them on the second ship. The ship sank, drowning several men.[45] If this was one of Franklin's ships, the incident must have happened after the original desertion of the ships, because Fitzjames' April 1848 addition to the note at the Victory Point cairn suggests that both *Erebus* and *Terror* were still beset. The implication was that some of the men may have gone back to the ships after the abandonment, and that *Terror* sank at that point.

Inuit hunters also told of a separate, perhaps even more intriguing incident. They talked of seeing a single ship of Franklin's after the encounter with the wandering party of men at Washington Bay, implying that it had been separated from its companion ship. Not only that, but they also saw evidence that men were living on this solitary ship. They saw fresh hard-soled footsteps of Europeans and a dog in the snow, and said they followed them to where the men killed a "deer." There were signs of life on the ship: the area around the ship was swept of snow, a plank had been set up from the deck to the ice as a walkway, a pile of dirt suggested the interior of the ship had been swept, smoke was coming from inside it and there was what might have been the remains of a cloth awning.[46]

These may have been clues about the last movements of the final survivors of the doomed 129 men. If they were, the dates suggest that some of Franklin's men were still alive when James Clark Ross was attempting to rescue them by ice sledge in May 1849.

The Inuit watched the ship for a long time—it is unclear how long—and when they didn't see evidence of any more movement or activity, one intrepid hunter went on board. Later, other Inuit did as well. Inside, they found a large man with big teeth, dead on the floor of a cabin at the back of the ship. They took a few artifacts from the ship. Some said they made a hole in the ship, but there are differing versions of this part of the tale. They all agreed that it sank.

McClintock heard a version of this story and even bought back some of the artifacts the Inuit said were taken from the ship. Hall, who lived with the Inuit for five years ending in 1869, also heard the story. So did Schwatka. So, many years later, did the modern historian Kamookak.

The key element to the tale is where it took place. It was not near the tip of King William Island where Franklin's 105 men abandoned their ships to the ice. It was farther south, in what the Inuit call Ookgoolik, the place of the bearded seals. It was near the continent's mainland, off Adelaide Peninsula, in Queen Maud Gulf, where the prime minister had just announced that the wreck of one of Franklin's vessels was found.

WONDER

S E P T E M B E R   1 7 – 1 8 ,   2 0 1 4

Q U E E N   M A U D   G U L F ,   A R C T I C   O C E A N

THE SEA WAS STILL AGITATED, forbidding, reluctant to relinquish her secrets. The divers, underwater archaeologists with Parks Canada, plunged in anyway, down eleven metres until they hit the ocean bottom. Nothing was visible, Marc-André Bernier, the head of the team, recounted later, just the milky brown hue of the Arctic water, churned by an angry wind.

Each diver in turn made his way forward, moving slowly through the gloom, so concentrated on the task that he didn't hear his own breath, hardly felt the cold. The men scanned the ocean floor, sweeping it with their eyes. Suddenly, a trail appeared. A few fractured timbers, lines softened by their time under the water. Then more. And then, looming in front of them, a dark shape, shrouded by the tumult of the water. It was massive. As tall as a two-storey building, lurking in the shadows of the ocean.

Closer yet. Closer. Then closer still. And then the wreck leapt out at them, her shape sharpening moment by moment. It was Franklin's ship, appearing as if in a dream to these men who had sought her for so long.

Each paused, Bernier said, forced by the weight of his own emotions to take stock of what it meant to be there, within reach of a ship no living human had touched for almost 170 years. So many had yearned to find her, to read her tantalizing tales, to savour them one by one. The men felt almost as if they were caught in a slow-motion trance, as if they had stumbled upon a secret world that wasn't supposed to exist.

It was a moment for philosophy. For parsing the trickster dimension of time that could make them feel as though the gap between that moment in 2014 and a century and a half before had collapsed. They felt as

With high winds stirring Queen Maud Gulf, the Underwater Archaeology Team was forced to wait out the weather. Each day of the delay, they held meetings planning the next day's dive, unsure if they'd be able to reach the wreck at all before the winter ice began to form.

Archaeologist Ryan Harris shares side-scan sonar images of HMS *Erebus* with the crew of CCGS *Sir Wilfrid Laurier* in the officers' lounge.

Archaeological work requires that each dive be carefully planned. Ryan Harris (with clipboard) discusses strategy with other members of the Underwater Archaeology Team at the wreck site of *Erebus* after the first dive.

if they had arrived there mere moments after the ship had settled on the ocean floor, shuddering, shedding small shards of her frame, locking herself away from the prying eyes of the world.

Still they paused, dragged reluctantly back to the present. For a few mesmerizing moments, they felt as though she had been waiting here patiently all these years, wanting to be found.

UP ON THE SURFACE, the underwater archaeologists on *Investigator* felt the pressure of a world of expectations. These modern explorers had finally tracked the scattered and cryptic clues left by Franklin's Victorian adventurers to find the ship, but so far, no one yet knew which ship it was. There was rampant speculation. Amateurs all over the world were clamouring to make their own identifications. That mystery, at least, had to be solved swiftly, if possible, and these archaeologists were the only ones in the world who could do so.

Not only that, but the divers also knew they had a slender window of time to be under the water with the wreck before the search wound down for the year. Already, the archaeologists had been right on top of the wreck for three fruitless days, waiting for the weather to improve enough to allow them to dive. The wind had made it too rough to get into the water. They felt that diving window closing inexorably.

It was frantic on another front, too. The archaeologists were feeling protective. *Erebus* and *Terror* were among the most famous wrecks anywhere in the world to resist discovery for so many years. The ship's find and its announcement had unleashed a torrent of attention in Canada and abroad. The allure for looters and thrill-seeking Franklin aficionados was strong. The Parks Canada team felt the responsibility to keep the ship secure from illicit divers, souvenir hunters and other possible interference until at least the first steps in the archaeological process were taken.

Not only that, but the ship was in such shallow water that it could be visible from the air if someone knew where to look and if the wind was low and the water clear. The team clamped down on information about precisely when and where the ship was found. The *Laurier* stopped sending out position information that would identify its coordinates around the time of the find so that outsiders couldn't figure it out.

She had rested there, lost but unmolested, for so many years—what if this wonderful discovery now made her vulnerable to damage? What if someone got to her before Parks Canada's own examination had really begun? The diving team imagined helicopters swooping in to spot the wreck from above. They envisioned scenarios of private yachts showing up unannounced and pillaging the site, even though they knew any ship would be risking ruin to go there, because the area is so poorly charted. Security had become the leading preoccupation.

Jonathan Moore points to a sketch plan of HMS *Erebus* as the Underwater Archaeology Team plans their next dives.

Jonathan Moore (left) looks on as the crew of *Sir Wilfrid Laurier* lowers *Investigator* onto Queen Maud Gulf in preparation to dive on the wreck of *Erebus*.

FINALLY, THE WIND HAD SETTLED, just enough. Under the murky water, Ryan Harris and Jonathan Moore, the first divers, were at last at the wreck doing the first reconnaissance. Their job was to commit to memory everything they saw so that the following dives could be tightly choreographed. Over the next two days, seven divers would spend a dozen hours examining the ship, taking photographs and hours of video, but for the moment, the main work was in their heads.

Every archaeological diver in the world wanted to be them at that moment. To members of their profession anywhere in the world, this was the holy grail, exploring this legendary, long-sought ship, sitting in impeccable shape. The momentous secrets still to be uncovered amplified the significance of everything they caught sight of. The questions the ship could resolve were shifting now that she had been found in such splendid condition.

Parks Canada underwater archaelogist Filippo
Ronca diving at the stern of HMS *Erebus*.

When examining kelp-covered shipwrecks like *Erebus*, archaeologists give the wreck a "haircut," gently and carefully trimming back growth so they can accurately catalogue what they find.

THIERRY BOYER/PARKS CANADA

They were taking in both the big picture and some of the fascinating smaller details, getting a clear record of how the ship looked at the moment of discovery. They noted how the wreck was resting on the sea floor, how much damage there was to the structure. The inspection was precise. Deliberate. Conservative. There is a code of honour among underwater archaeologists that they touch as little as possible at the beginning, that they proceed with exquisite caution. And this wreck was a prize to bask in.

The first thing Harris and Moore inspected was debris on the sea floor around the ship. There were rigging elements—that once held up masts and helped manoeuvre the sails—and parts of the three tall masts the sails once hung from, plus some yards that once spread the sails to catch the Arctic winds. From the look of them, they had been shorn off by the ferocious power of the ice. Most of the ship's wooden and iron pieces were obscured by sea life: great slippery swaths of kelp, or brown seaweed, and colonies of shelled creatures.

The debris field was strewn with anchors, perhaps half a dozen of them. That meant the anchors were on the deck when the ship sank, rather than tethered to the ship and nestled on the ocean floor, keeping the ship in one place. The archaeologists knew that it was one of the evocative new clues to the expedition's fate that they would be able to probe for meaning.

Harris and Moore continued to do the first circuit of the wreck. Harris swam to the back, the stern. Part of the vessel's structure had been torn away, as if a half-moon bite had been taken out of her. Moore was looking at the two guns first seen during the ROV dive. Then both of them ascended to the ship's upper deck and started moving slowly toward the front of the ship, the bow, peeking through holes in the barque's structure, gently pushing kelp aside, making meticulous mental notes. Harris ended up on the port side, the left as one looks to the bow, examining two patented brass Massey pumps, the newest innovation in 1845, installed on the ship to help keep the bilge water at bay. These pumps could be the only extant examples.

Parks Canada's Filippo Ronca dives along the midship section of the wreck of the *Erebus*, where the ship's hull meets the sea floor.

Moore was on the starboard side—to the right as one faces the bow. The two divers were talking to each other over radio, swimming parallel to each other, one on either side of the wreck, marvelling at these extraordinary treasures right there within reach for the first time in all these decades. The round drum of the capstan, which was used to wind heavy rope, standing up above the decking. The tiller, right on deck, a critical piece of the ship's steering apparatus. It would have been attached to the rudder underneath the stern at one end and to the helm by thick ropes at the other. The windlass, a type of horizontal winch for raising and lowering an anchor, thickly blanketed with kelp.

And then, Moore spotted it: something that stood out off in the distance on the upper deck.

It was green and slightly shiny, just catching the rays of his flashlight. It was one of the few items not covered in plant or animal life, a clue that it was made of a copper alloy such as bronze. Could it be something even more important, found on the first dive? He swam closer. Then, unmistakably, he saw that it was the ship's bronze bell, lying on its side, mouth open to the sea. Even from a distance, he could see its broad arrow. Ferociously excited, he swam closer, shining his light on it more directly and calling for Harris to join him.

The detached bell, as found on the upper deck of *Erebus*, next to the ship's windlass.

Spotted by Jonathan Moore during the first ever dive on *Erebus*, the ship's bell was embossed with a broad arrow and the date 1845, both of which were clearly visible underwater.

Moore got in close and, then, in front of him, above the arrow, no name, but the date, clear as the day the bell was cast in honour of Franklin's voyage: 1845. A career highlight. A huge find. The wild moment he will remember his whole life. He radioed to his colleagues on the boat above: "The bell! I found the bell!" He wiggled it slightly to see if it was corroded to the deck or whether it might easily come free. And then Harris appeared, the two of them savouring the moment of discovery of the bell from one of Franklin's ships.

FINDING THE BELL unleashed new worlds of possibilities about what secrets the ship might now be able to surrender. Could there be bodies? If the ship was a burial site as well as a wreck, then it would merit an even higher degree of historical significance and protection, Harris and Moore knew. Swimming around the ship during that first dive, they could already see that it would likely be possible to enter it safely to explore for corpses. Inuit accounts suggest that one body was on board the ship when she came to rest in Queen Maud Gulf—the remnants of a man with huge teeth, lying in a locked cabin. Harris and Moore knew that this was unlikely to be Franklin, even if it was there to be found. An officer of Franklin's stature would have been placed reverently in a formal coffin, buried at sea or on land. If on land, might this ship contain a detailed account of where Franklin's officers built his crypt, with a precise position describing its location that would lead modern explorers to it? Or were Franklin's remains carefully packed up and taken by the dying 105 men who left the ships, a bid to take their commander's remains back to Britain as naval tradition adjured?

Although their code of conduct would not have them disturb any human remains without the approval of the United Kingdom, the archaeologists knew that human remains could provide a gold mine of information. Forensic scientists could analyze them for clues about why Franklin's men made the decisions they did in the months following his death and the abandonment of the ships in April 1848. The divers couldn't help but think about what went so catastrophically wrong during those months. Perhaps this wreck contained unopened bright red tins of food that could be tested for lead, food poisoning and other substances. Could the officers, the expedition's navigators and those responsible for making decisions—who died in disproportionate numbers—have been more affected by lead poisoning because they ate more of a certain type of food?

Inside the body of the ship, deep in those hidden crevices they could peer into, were there maps and charts, ready to be discovered? What if they were literally frozen in time, preserved from the abrasions of the currents by the ice, the salt water, the lack of oxygen, the absence of light? And if they were, such tantalizing tales they might tell. Perhaps Franklin and his men believed that the ice would eventually release its grip on the ships and allow them to sail south to the coast of North America and then complete the Northwest Passage. Did Franklin die retaining hope, believing that the expedition could still be a success? Or had he succumbed to despair? Did his men march south on the island toward Back River after they abandoned ship, rather than north toward the whaling routes of Lancaster Sound, in order to complete the Northwest Passage? If so, were they following Franklin's commands even then?

What other documents might be there in those watery archives? The ship's logbooks? The journals of the prolific chronicler James Fitzjames? Might the officers have kept track of any encounters with Inuit? What about disturbing Inuit testimony given to Charles Francis Hall, describing men with blackened faces, hands and clothing who with terrifying cries seized an Inuit hunter as he boarded a ship locked in the ice? Could it be that a small group of the 105 survivors returned to the ships after they initially abandoned them and that the visit from the Inuit hunter is an unsettling vignette from that later time of disarray? Did Inuit hunters really witness *Terror* sink with men on her? Could there be a description of those dreadful final months in the obdurate clasp of the ice, as the officers must have struggled to retain control, discipline and even sanity?

Perhaps the ship contained evidence of the earlier, happier days of the voyage, of men studiously immersed in their intellectual quests. Like other expeditions of the Victorian era and before, Franklin's was primarily a geographical undertaking with a scientific purpose as well. That means officers would have collected samples of plants and animals, as Fitzjames's account of Harry Goodsir looking at his creatures under the microscope at the beginning of the voyage attests. Are those very samples stored on board with written records of how and when and where they were collected? Are there accounts of how many marine creatures the men saw during their voyage, how many they killed, how many they ate? Perhaps there is a unique biological snapshot of what lived in the Arctic lands and ocean in that period. Will modern biologists, schooled in the theories of evolution that Charles Darwin published in the same fateful year that Francis Leopold McClintock returned to Britain with word of Franklin's fate, be able to learn anything new about how the Arctic functioned then?

Hauntingly, what if the cabins the divers were scanning within the ship's viscera contained silver-covered metallic plates from the daguerreotype machine—akin to early film photographs—still capable of offering up their images? Such a richness of Victorian-era shipboard detail might live on in those images. Could those daguerreotype images have captured the shocking unravelling of the expedition, and might they chronicle the scurvy and starvation of the men? Or would the images have preserved only the semblance of naval order and discipline that the Admiralty would have approved? Might the daguerreotypist have captured images of *Erebus* and *Terror* locked in the ice, taken from the frozen sea? Images of any sort would inflame the public imagination, as did the photographs Owen Beattie and his team took of the corpses of the first three of Franklin's men to die, buried and later exhumed for autopsy and then reburied on Beechey Island.

The questions were endless. Which answers would the ship deign to relinquish? Which would she keep to herself?

✛

ONCE THE FIRST HOUR of diving was over for Harris and Moore, Thierry Boyer and Filippo Ronca took their place, followed by Bernier and Charles Dagneau, and then Joe Boucher with Harris again. Chriss Ludin, *Investigator*'s captain and the team's senior technician, kept a close eye on the boat and weather conditions. With each moment under water, with each photograph and frame of video, they refined the picture, filling in more and more detail. They spied a crushed box-like piece of metal. Two six-pound brass cannons. This was a fascinating glimpse into the mind of the Victorian engineer, pieces of beautifully preserved Victorian machinery.

Parks Canada's Filippo Ronca shines a light on the bell of HMS *Erebus* before it was lifted to the surface.

Thierry Boyer/Parks Canada

The Parks Canada archaeologists knew that the ship would be able to answer questions not only about the fate of Franklin's men but also about the physical plant of the ship. The ship is a trove of information about the history of shipbuilding and expeditions. How did all that advanced Victorian technology, designed to help the ship withstand the Arctic ice and work through it, ultimately fare during Franklin's voyage? How did it protect her during her long sojourn trapped in the ice?

Did the grinding ice damage the ship's many structural reinforcements? She already boasted a robust body. Years ago, before she set sail on a voyage to Antarctica in 1839, shipwrights had added a second layer of planking to her hull, later plated with iron at the bow to help her withstand ice blows and pressure from outside. Does it show the terrible force of the ice she was trapped in? Did the thick crossbeams, strengthened with iron braces, start to twist or break during her ordeal? Are the huge, thick pieces of felted wool in between the planks still helping to protect her in the frigid Arctic waters where she now rests?

And what about the train engine and propeller? A propeller was a revolutionary idea at the end of the age of

sail, put in place to help the ship move—albeit slowly at about seven and a half kilometres an hour—when advantageous, and only sparingly given the limited amount of coal she carried. Francis Crozier, who was rather dour, as historians know, disliked the idea of an engine on his ship and wrote to an acquaintance that he wished it were back on its train. Did the propeller see service? Will the archaeologists find indications of whether this novel propulsion system functioned well, if, indeed, it was used? Was it continually being mended during the expedition?

The sonar images that the archaeologists have been poring over show that some of the planking on the upper deck has fallen away, including pieces of the topmost, diagonal layer designed to absorb the pressure of ramming ice. Did the planks loosen and fall when the ship sank, or might they have been damaged before?

What was her fatal flaw, in the end? Did the Inuit really bash a hole in the ship that led to her sinking? Did the wood simply become too stressed to withstand the strain of the ice any longer? Why did she sink in Queen Maud Gulf after defying the ice of Victoria Strait for at least two winters? Was she perhaps embedded in an ice floe, damaged and carried south, safe until the floe melted in Queen Maud Gulf, but once freed, so overcome by her injuries that she sank in the water where she now rests?

＋

EACH OF THE DIVERS caught sight of the bell in his turn, up there on the kelp-infested deck. It is impossible to see the bell of a wreck and not imagine a captain. The captain—Franklin himself, or later Fitzjames, or perhaps Crozier—would have used the bell to muster the men to tell them the news: someone had died; someone was being punished; the ship was stuck in the ice; food supplies were running low; they were abandoning ship. All of the drama happened right there on deck.

And the deck was where the emotion caught them, all seven men who dived there over those two days. The deck of a sailing ship is its theatre of action, both day and night. Here, the captain barked out commands in the naval argot, ordering the crew to set or strike a specific combination of the complex array of sails. The sailors scampered to obey him so the ship could catch a breath of wind or avoid one, or even slip into a disappearing path in the ice. They heaved on the heavy ropes to set the sails just so and fixed them, wound the ropes into perfectly shaped coils when their extent was not needed, clambered the masts to free tangled lines and sails as necessary, secured the sails when they were down, lowered the anchors, ritually swabbed and polished the deck according to a rigid schedule set down by centuries of marine protocol. The archaeologist divers knew the discipline, the precision, the art that running a vessel like this one would have taken.

It was like travelling back in time to see that ancient deck. It felt as though if the divers waited just a few moments more, the sailors would appear, clad in their navy blues, neckerchiefs jaunty, intent on their work. And then some of the divers looked down into the ship's interior, taking brief glimpses of the very lower deck Franklin's men had walked, into the open area where most would have slept and eaten. Again, the emotion was palpable. They could imagine how the ship had appeared before it had been abruptly abandoned.

BOTH EVENINGS AFTER the two days of diving, gathered in *Laurier*'s laboratory or lounge, the divers pored over their growing stash of riches: every photograph, each moment of the video, each memory, reliving every second of each dive. It was revelation upon revelation. Their high-definition cameras had lighting systems and aperture settings that far exceed the capabilities of the human eye. Even diver Boyer, who took the shots, was astonished at what they contained. They would minutely examine one segment of a frame when, suddenly, in a different portion of it, another image would appear, unseen until then, developing like a Polaroid picture right under their eyes. It was exhilarating.

Their imaginations took flight. What if men got back on board after the order to evacuate and begin the march to Back River? Could the amount of coal still contained on the ship offer any new analysis? Was any of it used to heat discrete portions of the vessel? The amount of food—if any—remaining on the ship when she sank could indicate the degree of starvation the men endured. Could there be evidence that the crew hunted and fished for fresh meat during the expedition or later, during a re-manning of the vessel? Are there pieces of clothing or other identifying items that could provide hints about which sailors might have returned or remained on board? Perhaps Crozier or Fitzjames or another of the officers was among them.

If some of the crew returned to the ship after the original abandonment, will it be possible to tell from their remains, if any, whether they participated in the march of death down King William Island and then turned back? If they turned back, why did they do so? Perhaps the men McClintock and William Hobson found in the modified sledge-boat on the western shore of the island were part of a party of men returning to the ships. If men returned to the ships, did the ice eventually free the ship long enough for the men to attempt to steer or sail her south to the continent's jagged northern shore? Should proof emerge that Franklin's men were on the ship, would that lead to the astonishing revelation that they had symbolically completed the Northwest Passage after all, joining the final few kilometres of unexplored water and land to make the route whole? This would represent a wholesale rewriting of the history books.

Or did the ice simply carry the ship south, creeping slowly, as the Canadian Ice Service's Thomas Zagon's modern ice analysis suggests?

If men reboarded the ship and lived on her while she made her way south, did they then abandon her a second time when she came to rest in Queen Maud Gulf, where she eventually sank? Could there be a second trail of abandonment to investigate? Perhaps some of the clues that explorers have been tracking for more than a century and a half are signs of unexpected activity.

Could it be that a small band of Franklin's men, wandering in the general area of Queen Maud Gulf and separated from those on the final march, stumbled across the ship adrift in the sea or locked in ice farther to the south than they had left her? Did they get on her again—in amazement—at that time?

Sections of the ship's upper deck lie on the sea floor surrounding the ship's hull. Here a section of the two-layer deck planking can be seen. Two holes for below-deck glass illuminators (one round and one rectangular) are visible.

Arctic diving is cold, but water temperatures in Queen Maud Gulf are comparable to more southerly locations where the Underwater Archaeology Team works, such as Red Bay, Labrador, and the waters of the Gulf of St. Lawrence.

✦

ON A FUNDAMENTAL archival level, excavation is destruction. Once done, it cannot be undone. Ever after, the archaeologists will have only these records they have made of how things were. And Bernier is all too conscious of the intrusiveness of the process. He has described the excavation of a shipwreck as "like reading a book, but the pages disappear as you read it, so if you don't take notes and record everything, that story is gone." Not only that, but it's also like reading a book from the end, he has said, peeling off everything that has been deposited on the ship in the past century and a half to get at what remains underneath.

That means that however much information might be contained in goods or materials lodged on the ship, Bernier and the other divers immersed in the photographs and video on *Laurier* knew that the first phases of archaeological investigation would not include removing them. Long before that is even contemplated comes the hands-off, extensive surveying and documentation of the ship that was begun during the first dives. The placement of items can give a glimpse into precisely how the ship settled on the seabed, for example. If excavation were to ever happen, like all archaeological work, it would be done with precision and discipline, much like the process of conducting a scientific experiment or manoeuvring a navy sailing ship. Eventually, reams of academic articles published in peer-reviewed scholarly journals are bound to enhance the international body of knowledge of the science of archaeology.

First, the thronged patches of seaweed would be carefully clipped back, never torn away, because their roots are strong enough that they could tear pieces of the ship away. Any artifacts are bound to be fragile. The team would likely set up a shipboard conservation laboratory, possibly on *Martin Bergmann,* before taking artifacts to the Parks Canada lab in Ottawa.

Every artifact would be X-rayed. In some cases when iron-based material has been suspended in salt water for a long time, the iron leaches out to form concretions, rock-like substances that can contain hidden treasures. One concretion from a different wreck hid a human hair of great importance; others have contained ceramic, glass or leather.

The waterlogged timbers would merit special consideration. Their cells, replete with salt water, would become unstable and collapse once the timbers were removed from the water and the water evaporated. Then the wood would twist, an archaeological catastrophe. To avoid that, the conservators would replace the water with a more stable liquid, often polyethylene glycol, immersing the artifact in the liquid for sometimes years on end. One worry is that the wood might leach sulphuric acid, which, in turn, could corrode and even destroy the metal fasteners on the wood.

Bernier and the others had already been repeatedly asked the biggest question of all: whether to raise the ship once the excavation is complete—assuming excavation takes place. Marine archaeologists have a noble tradition of raising and restoring wrecks. But today, leaving wrecks in place—in situ—is the preferred option, according to the UNESCO convention on underwater heritage. It's not just the astronomical cost of raising and restoring a vessel such as one of Franklin's—certainly tens of millions of dollars over forty to fifty years—or the technical difficulties of dealing with wood soaked in salt water for more than 160 years that are challenging. It's also that if the ship were removed from her final resting place, it would be difficult for the public to imagine what the men endured in their final days. That sense of place would be lost forever.

Breadalbane, a barque sent to the Arctic in 1853 to provision one of the many expeditions looking for Franklin, is one of the relatively recent finds to be left where she lies. She became caught in the ice just south of Beechey Island, was crushed and then sank. Her crew survived. She was discovered in 1980 by the Canadian Arctic diving pioneer, explorer and physician Joe MacInnis. Yet other vessels have been resurrected, proving to be superb tourist attractions and ongoing scholarly research sites. British scientists raised *Mary Rose*, King Henry VIII's Tudor flagship, which sank in 1545 with more than four hundred sailors on board. After thirty years of restoration, the ship and nineteen thousand of its artifacts are now on display in Portsmouth. The ship receives 400,000 visitors a year, and scientific papers continue to be published on her findings, including a recent paper describing the extent of rickets evident in the bones of the sailors who went down. The Swedish ship *Vasa*, raised 333 years after she sank just outside the Stockholm harbour on her maiden

Nunavut archaeologist Douglas Stenton (right) examines the bell of HMS *Erebus* in a lab on board the CCGS *Sir Wilfrid Laurier* with Ryan Harris and Jonathan Moore of Parks Canada.

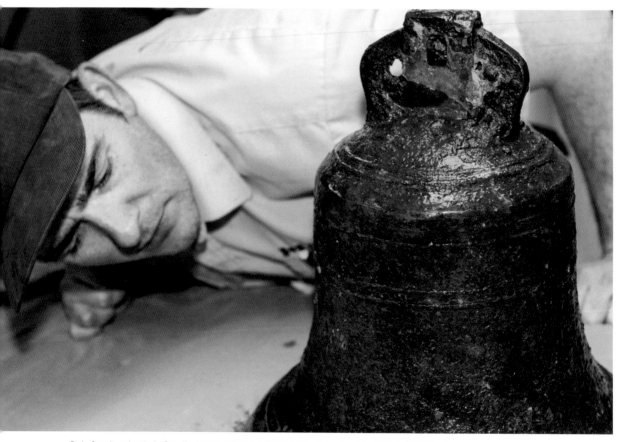

Parks Canada archaeologist Ryan Harris studies the bell of HMS *Erebus* in a lab on board the CCGS *Sir Wilfrid Laurier*.

voyage, is now on display in a dedicated building. It is Sweden's most popular museum, attracting more than a million visitors a year.

But while *Mary Rose* and *Vasa* are intriguing in their own rights, neither has the enduring mystery of a vessel from Franklin's doomed expedition. There will be immense longing from the public to see her, to lay human hands on her once more, to understand what drama she witnessed all those years ago and perhaps to catch a glimpse of the ghosts who may walk her still.

✦

IT WAS SEPTEMBER 18, 2014, and *Laurier* had to head back to Cambridge Bay. That meant the expedition had to come to an end. The archaeologists had had only two days of diving and now they had to leave the ship where she lay. It was torment. They had already had a taste of the mysteries she contained. Now they would have to wait until the following year to probe her secrets again.

Moore and Dagneau entered the water for the bittersweet final dive. Theirs was the trickiest part of the dive mission: bringing up the ship's bell from the depths.

It is a highly symbolic act to bring up a bell, a hallowed part of any underwater recovery. Rear Admiral John Newton said the bell is the essence of a ship. He pointed to the wreck of SS *Edmund Fitzgerald*, which sank in 1975 with no survivors, the largest ship to have been lost to the Great Lakes. Its bell was recovered and replaced by a replica inscribed with the names of the twenty-nine who perished on her and were never found. Even today, Newton said, the bell on navy ships is turned upside down to serve as a baptismal font when the crew's children are christened. The holy water is then poured back into the sea and the child's name engraved on the bell.

The bell of this ship was her soul and perhaps her heart. It was certainly her inflexible time-keeper. It would have summoned the men to their shifts and their prayers, marked the start of their meals, the passing of the hours and the days. It was the feared regulator of the crew's life and there was no negotiating with it. What the bell demanded, it got. It is the ultimate artifact. If a museum of Franklin artifacts is established in Canada, this bronze bell will form a centrepiece of it. Given its importance, the Parks Canada team began to carefully consider raising this iconic object right after the first dive, a step they discussed extensively with archaeologist Douglas Stenton.

Harris had begun to suspect that this was Franklin's own ship, *Erebus*, based on subtle clues from measurements and construction details. As Moore and Dagneau were beginning the final dive, they had to wonder: Was this Franklin's bell? Might Franklin's hands have touched its surface, rung its toll? Did his commands make it call out to his men? Did it toll on the day he died?

The divers had only a single hour to get the bell to the surface. Together, Moore and Dagneau had spent hours meticulously choreographing the dive and had consulted with Parks Canada conservation experts about the most scientifically correct ways to release the bell from its resting place and get it to the surface

HMS *Erebus* was outfitted with a new bell the year it sailed on its final expedition. It is not known if this was because of the expedition's prestige or because something happened to the ship's previous bell.

without damage. They had already prepared bandages so they could bundle the bell like a baby in swaddling clothes before it rose, and had commissioned a bespoke wooden crate to be built to transport it south. They were fighting the clock. The weather was still wretched and *Laurier* captain Bill Noon had given a strict time limit for *Investigator* to return to the ship. They knew they wouldn't have another chance that year to retrieve the prize.

Carefully they wrapped the bell in the bandages, placed it into a net scavenged from *Laurier*'s hold and then secured it to a sling. Then very carefully, they attached a lifting bag and began to inflate it with air from their diving gear. They then moved it over to a rope and lifting tackle lowered from *Investigator*'s stern. Painstakingly slowly, the bell was raised from the deck, severed now from the body of its ship, swaying slightly in the ocean until it hit the air for the first time in more than a century and a half.

And then the expedition was over for the year, to be resumed months later. The archaeologists got aboard *Investigator*, back over to *Laurier*, and then they all boarded aircraft to fly home, knowing that untold discoveries from this astonishing vessel are still down there, enticing, waiting for the next archaeological investigation.

This broad arrow embossed on the bell of HMS *Erebus* marks it as property of the Royal Navy.

Thierry Boyer/Parks Canada

This three-dimensional model of HMS *Erebus* was made using multibeam sonar. Operated by the Canadian Hydrographic Service, the technology is primarily used to chart the ocean floor.

CONFIRMATION

SEPTEMBER 30, 2014

OTTAWA

BUT WHICH SHIP HAD THEY FOUND? *Erebus* or *Terror*? Despite all the measurements and observations they had made while they were diving, the archaeologists couldn't be absolutely certain. Social media and Franklin aficionados were already claiming to know the truth, based on slim and nonexistent evidence; unofficial announcements were racing across the Internet. The theories about which one it would turn out to be reached far back into the Victorian age, into the rescue and recovery voyages that so many had undertaken in the decades right after Franklin's ships had vanished into thin air. They reached back into the accounts of the Inuit who came across Franklin's dying and dead men, Inuit who said they saw a ship in the area where Harris and his men had been diving on the wreck, and into the translations of those accounts and their interpretation over the many decades since.

Harris made it his personal quest to make the ultimate determination. The archaeologist knew he would have to have multiple points of confirmation. He would not make the identification without absolute certainty. He was intimately aware of the historical record and also of the revelations from Zagon's modern analysis of the ice regime of the past several years. He and Zagon had concluded that one of Franklin's ships could well have made it to this part of the Arctic Ocean, carried excruciatingly slowly by ice.

But which one? Either would, of course, be an incalculable prize. But by far the more important of the two ships was *Erebus*, Franklin's own. *Erebus* would hold the answers to far more of the mysteries.

So Harris was doing what archaeologists do. Back in Ottawa, he was going to the archive, to the testimony of papers and records, to copies of ink-drawn Victorian plans of both *Erebus* and *Terror*, lodged with

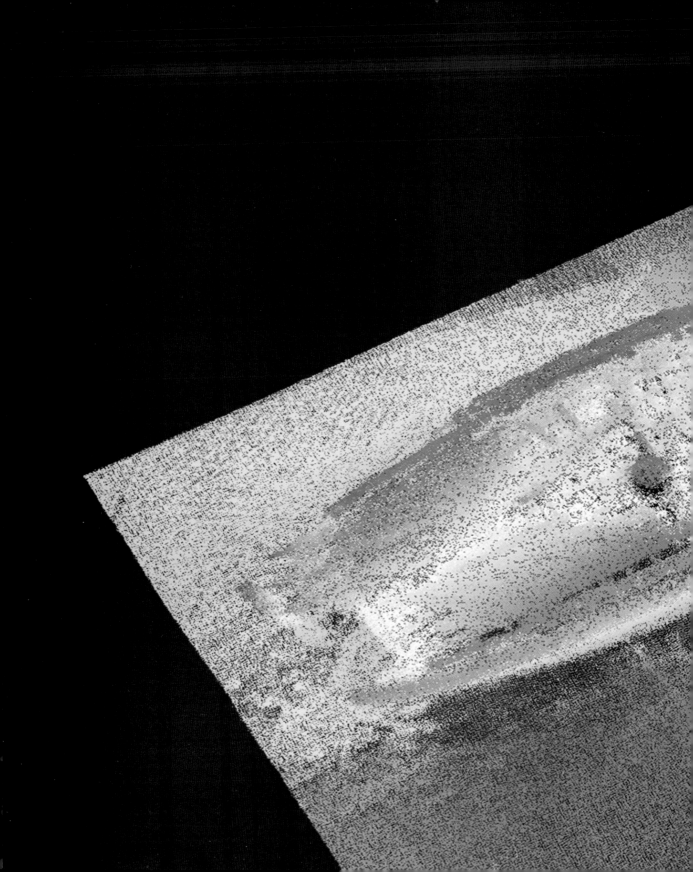

This colourful image of HMS *Erebus* was created by the
Canadian Hydrographic Service using multibeam sonar.

the National Maritime Museum in Greenwich, England. He was comparing the time-worn plans of the two ships, noting minute differences between them. It was complex, meticulous work. Each of the ships had been through many refurbishments over her years of service, and there were different sets of plans as a result. *Erebus* and *Terror* were both originally bomb vessels, and they were very similar, but, built thirteen years apart, they were not precisely the same proportions. Then Harris scrutinized multibeam sonar images that the Canadian Hydrographic Service had produced of the wreck. They were almost unimaginably detailed.

Painstakingly, Harris superimposed the modern sonar images over each set of scrupulously drawn Victorian ink plans, deck by deck, millimetre by millimetre. The outer dimensions. The inner dimensions. The proportions of each part of the ship. Where the masts were placed, and the hatches. The shape of the windlass. Every metal eye bolt. A perfectionist, he even checked the placement of the illuminators—circular prisms set precisely between the deck beams to shoot light into lower levels, akin to a Victorian central lighting system.

Finally, he had made all the calculations. Only one set of ink-drawn plans fit perfectly. Every detail was precise. Without a doubt, this was *Erebus*, Franklin's own ship. The more important of the two. It was an immense discovery. This was the biggest breakthrough anyone could have imagined.

Erebus had been found at last.

CAPTAIN FRANKLIN.

LONDON:
Published by William Wright.

EPILOGUE

THE AGE OF CHANGE

FOR MORE THAN A CENTURY AND A HALF, the fate of the lost ships of Sir John Franklin was the most enduring mystery of the North. The mystery was enhanced by the Victorian notion of the Arctic as the idealized, romantic land that time forgot, fixed in snow, frozen in ice, immutable. That haughty resistance to change rendered the North alluring, ripe for the challenge of conquest, even as it remained unconquered.

So perhaps it is fitting that just as Franklin's lost flagship, *Erebus*, is finally found and its mysteries begin to be solved, so, too, are the Arctic's own mysteries yielding to human knowledge. As technology advances, as the world becomes more globalized, as the climate warms and the ice melts, the Arctic itself is changing in ways unimaginable even a few decades ago. Today, cruise ships sail through the Northwest Passage every year, and so do private yachts. For several years during the past decade, the passage has been free of ice in the late summer.

The sea route to the Orient that industrialists and traders have dreamed of for more than five hundred years is becoming possible, even as Asian markets are clamouring for the raw goods the rest of the world can provide. Such a trade route has rarely been more desirable. While the summer of 2014's events showed that new ice can come back in part of the passage for a while, the larger trend is for a deep and ultimately permanent melt. In fact, despite the ice of that summer, a commercial ship was able to ferry minerals out of the Arctic and deliver them to China through the Northwest Passage—without needing an icebreaker. This is another game-changer. Industrial development of the High North is a topic of fervent discussion among Inuit and non-Inuit.

The changes mean that more people are travelling to the Arctic now than at any previous time. The Arctic, once the ultimate in impenetrability, is becoming more knowable, more known, more welcoming. Its secrets are being revealed.

Stephen Pearce's painting *The Arctic Council Planning a Search for Sir John Franklin* shows early searchers planning their attempt to locate signs of the Franklin expedition. From left to right: The Royal Navy's Sir George Back, Sir William Edward Parry, Edward Joseph Bird, Sir James Clark Ross, Sir Francis Beaufort, archivist to the Admiralty John Barrow, the Royal Society's Edward Sabine, the Royal Navy's William Alexander Baillie Hamilton, explorer Sir John Richardson and the Royal Navy's Frederick William Beechey.

Prior to the Victoria Strait Expedition, some of its key members gathered in Ottawa to recreate Stephen Pearce's 1851 painting *The Arctic Council Planning a Search for Sir John Franklin*. From left to right: David Hopkin of Defence Research and Development Canada, Douglas Stenton of the Government of Nunavut, George Schlagintweit of the Canadian Hydrographic Service, Jim Balsillie of the Arctic Research Foundation, Prime Minister Stephen Harper, Andrew Prossin of One Ocean Expeditions, Peter Koch of National Defence, Geordie Dalglish of The W. Garfield Weston Foundation, The Royal Canadian Geographical Society CEO John Geiger, and Environment Minister Leona Aglukkaq.

1 Canadian Ranger Patrol Group Ranger Hennery Lyall from Taloyoak, Nunavut, waves goodbye as the Canadian Armed Forces' Twin Otter 803 prepares to take off after dropping off a generator and other gear at the site of HMS *Erebus* on April 9, 2015.

THE FRANKLIN STORY has crept slowly into Canada's cultural landscape and its political life. For the first century, it was quintessentially British, as the Canadian novelist Margaret Atwood noted in her Oxford lectures in 1991. But gradually, after Canada became a country in 1867, Canadians who were not Inuit began to claim the tale and even to shape it. "Later on, when Canada was beginning to identify its very own nightmares, the Franklin expedition was among them," Atwood noted.[47]

The stuff of the Canadian nightmares revolved around imagery of the mystic, alluring, sometimes sinister North, hostile, unconquerable, and frequently fatal to non-Inuit like Franklin, she said. "It would lead you on and do you in . . . drive you crazy, and, finally, would claim you for its own."[48]

As for generations of British, the emerging non-Inuit Canadian fascination with Franklin had its roots in

Parks Canada's lead archaeologist Ryan Harris (left) and senior underwater archaeologist Jonathan Moore verify the positioning of one of the ice holes next to *Erebus* using an underwater video camera held by Royal Canadian Navy Fleet Diving Unit Atlantic clearance diving officer Lieutenant Greg Oickle.

One of the first tasks at the dive site in April 2015 was to make the holes in the ice for dives on *Erebus*. Here, Jonathan Moore uses a Defence Research and Development Canada hot-water drill to make one side of a triangular dive hole.

the mythology of the Northwest Passage. The passage was not so much a place or a topographical reality to most British as it was a rich metaphor. For British politicians ranging back to the fifteenth century, the passage represented an opportunity to establish and expand the Empire, to convince other nations of its global dominance, its naval superiority. Culturally, it meant supremacy over nature, derring-do, romantic quests, money, power, glory. When all that began to pale after the crushing loss of Franklin, Britain eventually transferred responsibility for its Arctic properties to Canada.

As the Canadian polar historian Shelagh Grant explained in an article in *Canadian Geographic* magazine,[49] Canada was originally too immersed in settling the West and establishing its agricultural wealth on the Prairies to bother with the Arctic or the Northwest Passage. It wasn't until the twentieth century that it established sovereign title to the area.

But the metaphor persisted. Atwood tracked one powerful strand of it that has withstood time: the Northwest Passage as a feat of the imagination. Humans invented it; humans endowed it with meaning. And that invention bore directly on Franklin's expedition.

"This point of view—that the imagination and will invent reality—has a corollary: if it was a success of the imagination that 'created' the Passage it was a failure of the imagination that created the failure of the expedition itself," Atwood suggested.[50]

And perhaps more than political leaders of other eras, Prime Minister Stephen Harper attached his country's national sense of self to this rich metaphor that is Franklin's quest, that is the Northwest Passage, that is the North. However, the meaning of this set of metaphors has shifted over time, protean as the ice. Now the narrative is not about defeat. It is about triumph. Franklin's ship is found at last, and with Canadian and Inuit expertise, no less. It is a poetic hearkening back to the words of Mary Shelley's character in *Frankenstein*: "This ice cannot withstand you if you say that it shall not."

Except today, those words seem spookily prophetic. The Arctic is becoming less remote, less forbidding.

No longer is it murderous and nightmarish. It is what the West used to be: ripe. The fabled path to the Orient is no longer just a fantasy; it is becoming a reality. As a result, others want in. The United States sees the Northwest Passage as an international waterway rather than Canada's sovereign inland waters. Resource riches also attract. Denmark recently added its claim to the North Pole to existing claims from Canada and Russia.

And that means now, in Harper's political narrative, Canada must protect what is quintessentially its own, must safeguard its identity from those who would try to wrest it away.

The need to quickly follow up the discovery with further investigations of *Erebus* was clear. As part of Operation Nunalivit, which involved 200 personnel and was commanded by Joint Task Force North, Parks Canada underwater archaeologists and the Royal Canadian Navy's Fleet Diving Unit Atlantic dove under the Arctic sea ice in April 2015 to study the wreck.

Navy clearance divers lift an ice block from the dive hole with a sled.

MASTER SEAMAN PETER REED

BUT EVEN AS CHANGE RESHAPES the mystique of the Arctic and the Northwest Passage—embodied in the find of *Erebus*—the region is tethered to the past. Its ancient tales poignantly meld with the new.

Historically, a major reason stated for traversing the Northwest Passage was rather workmanlike: to find a shorter trade route. This is echoed in the discourse about today's possibilities for shipping. But then, as now, the quest was grander and more poetic than those stated goals; the Northwest Passage has always been a metaphor for the human ability to dream, to defy the odds, to prevail against expectation.

In Franklin's day, the bid to complete the passage was urged on by the scientific need to advance the "magnetic

Jonathan Moore (right) and Parks Canada underwater archaeologist and lead photo-video specialist Thierry Boyer use an underwater camera to check on the position of a second diving hole.

MASTER SEAMAN PETER REED

crusade," or to understand how the Earth works as a magnet with two poles. Scientists were ardently searching for ways to adjust compass anomalies that intensified near the magnetic North and South Poles. Geomagnetism was the most exciting scientific inquiry of the day, and only the poles held the potential of answering it. *Erebus* and *Terror* were both involved in geomagnetic research in Antarctica under the command of Captain James Clark Ross, prior to embarking on their Arctic explorations. Franklin set up a geomagnetic outpost in the Arctic before his expedition took its fatal turn. In fact, it was only with the publication of Charles Darwin's work *On the Origin of Species* in 1859 that the scientific lens turned resolutely away from geomagnetism and toward the biological mysteries of the planet.

✦

OTHER LINKS BETWEEN the past and today have to do with the geographical imagination. In the Victorian age, British explorers were searching for the first glimpses of the Arctic Archipelago, attempting to map the islands' quizzical boundaries and claim both land and sea for the British Empire, and trying to do it all before the Americans or explorers of any other nation could get there. It had to do with global mastery, with building the Empire, with proving the might of the British.

And the quest for the Northwest Passage was the main mechanism for conducting those charting expeditions, using the most advanced naval technology that existed—that is, until Franklin and his two ships went missing. After his disappearance, the extended series of searches to find Franklin—three dozen under several national flags just to the end of 1859—vastly and swiftly expanded the knowledge of the Arctic's islands and shorelines. It's been said that nothing developed the Arctic's cartographic archive as much as the loss of Franklin's doomed voyage.

Canadian Rangers and a navy diver look into the dive hole where a seal made an appearance.

THIERRY BOYER/PARKS CANADA

Thierry Boyer gets dressed with the assistance of Jonathan Moore and underwater archaeology technician Joe Boucher before a dive on the wreck in April 2015.

MASTER SEAMAN PETER REED, FORMATION IMAGING SERVICES, HALIFAX, DND

To work beneath the ice with navy divers like Yves Bernard, shown here, Parks Canada's Underwater Archaeology Team had to be trained in surface supply diving techniques. In the past, they've worked with scuba gear.

Parks Canada underwater archaelogy technician Joe Boucher shines a light on the wreck of HMS *Erebus* during the April 2015 dive beneath the Arctic ice.

Today, efforts to find Franklin's lost ships are playing a similar role in the continued mapping of the Arctic. But now, the mapping is mainly focused on the vagaries of the ocean floor and the critical contours of the underwater continental shelf. So far, most Arctic waters are uncharted, and so are the northernmost reaches of Canada's underwater borders. The search crews from the Arctic Research Foundation's *Martin Bergmann*, the only ship dedicated entirely to the Franklin quest, found that out first-hand in the days before *Erebus* was found. The ship was searching Queen Maud Gulf, not too far from where *Erebus* now lies, when, despite all her experience in that part of the Arctic, she hit an uncharted shoal in the wee hours of the morning. The ship couldn't pry herself loose for two and a half hours before finally freeing herself using her anchor as a winch.

But while the nineteenth-century geographical quest was to cement world dominance by grasping the Arctic prize, the twenty-first-century equivalent is for each Arctic nation to determine the limits of its own boundaries and resolve any simmering disputes over sovereignty. The mechanism is to methodically map the edges of the continental shelves of national territories and send those measurements to the United Nations, notes Rob Huebert, a political scientist at the University of Calgary who specializes in Arctic

Before joining Parks Canada for winter dives on the *Erebus*, navy clearance divers like Ryan Burrell (pictured here) were given archaeological training.

THIERRY BOYER/PARKS CANADA

security. That body will then assess each country's measurements and any overlap, and ultimately discern the extent of each nation's mineral and fishing rights. Rather than geopolitical bragging rights, this is about potential income from resources.

As in Franklin's age, Arctic exploration takes the latest technology and is fiendishly challenging. But today, instead of wooden warships retrofitted against the ice and armed with all the finest navigational equipment, the geographical tools are autonomous vehicles that can stay under the water, searching with high-resolution sonar in wide swaths for days at a time, aided by satellite data about ice movements. And while these sophisticated underwater vehicles will play a significant role in the ongoing searches for Franklin's second ship, *Terror*, they will also be used in the task of mapping the sea floor and the extent of Canada's underwater continental shelf. In fact, Huebert says it's clear that the Franklin search has helped spur the

The bow of the wreck of *Erebus* showing Roman numeral draught mark *XX* on the ship's stem (denoting 20 feet above the keel) partly covered by protective iron plating. The partial remains of mark *XXI* (21 feet) are visible above.

THIERRY BOYER/PARKS CANADA

testing of the technology necessary for the eventual mapping of the extent of Canada's maritime seabed and its legal bid to declare its boundaries. Both Franklin's original expedition and the modern search for his lost ships have helped push the frontiers of science and technology.

But the echoes reverberate beyond the industrial, the scientific and the technological. The find of *Erebus* signals a poetic geopolitical turnaround. When Franklin set off in 1845 and for the three and a half decades after, the Arctic and the Northwest Passage were notionally part of the British Empire. In 1880, fatigued with the Franklin drama, Britain handed its northern claims over to Canada, a pubescent teenager of a country at thirteen. Now that a robust Canadian public and private team has found *Erebus* using Canadian expertise, it is as if, finally, Canada and the Arctic have joined as rightful equals, rather than being thrust together by their colonial masters.

The symbols marking this turnaround infused the Victoria Strait Expedition that discovered *Erebus*. Parks

A closer look at the *XX* draught marks and iron plating.

The ship's main mast with the port side Massey pump in front of it.

Canada manages a network of national parks, national historic sites and national marine conservation areas across Canada, some of which are found in the Arctic. A Canadian Coast Guard ship patrolling Canada's Arctic waters was the mother vessel of the search and carried Canadian Hydrographic Service launches surveying its waters and helping to create new navigational charts. Scientists with the Canadian Ice Service monitored and mapped ice for the safety of navigation and kept an eye on conditions for searchers. There were no longer Royal Navy ships on the quest, but Royal Canadian Navy ships. It was a handing over, of sorts. A coming of age.

In the Victorian era, Franklin and his officers believed they could voyage to the land of the Inuit and survive on British wits alone—largely ignoring the wisdom of a people who had learned to live on the ice.

Today, Franklin's lost ship was found by Canadian scientists following their fellow Canadians' Inuit wisdom about where the ship sank. This was a fundamental co-operation between Inuit and non-Inuit in a territory of Canada, Nunavut, that is governed by Inuit. Not only that, but the Canadian federal government minister whose department was in charge of the search was Leona Aglukkaq, an Inuk who comes from Gjoa Haven, the Inuit community on King William Island, where Franklin's men marched to their death. From the beginning to the end of the modern search for *Erebus*, Inuit were involved in critical roles and the success relied on their expertise.

Detail of hull planking on the port side, around midship, showing copper tacks left after the removal of copper sheeting.

THIERRY BOYER/PARKS CANADA

On the body of the cannon is engraved the cipher of King George III: the letters *GR* encircled by the motto *Honi soit qui mal y pense* ("Shame on him who thinks this evil") topped by a crown.

One of the cannons from HMS *Erebus* is lifted through ice more than two metres thick.

Hoisting the cannon to the surface took careful planning and execution. The ice hole through which it would pass is visible above.

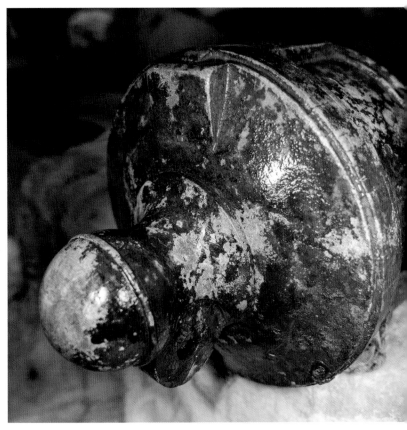

The cannon cascabel.

Designed to fire a six-pound projectile, this "brass six-pounder" was listed among the three guns that sailed with *Erebus* in 1845. It is in excellent condition and its many markings are surprisingly easy to read. The inscription "I&H King — 1812" reveals that it was cast by John and Henry King at the Royal Brass Foundry at Woolwich in 1812, while the inscription "6-0-8" indicates that the gun weighed a total of six hundredweight plus eight pounds, or 680 pounds (309 kilograms) in total.

✦

PERHAPS THE LARGER MEANING of the find of *Erebus* is that it could not have happened until now, until the peoples of Canada, northerners and southerners, and multiple layers of government and non-governmental organizations and the private sector could collaborate so freely. This is the modern Canadian national identity that prides itself on fostering an inclusive, curious society. It's the emerging metaphor of the Arctic as it becomes a more central part of the Canadian psyche: pushing on together against all odds to create something no one else could create.

Erebus lost is solitude and fracture. *Erebus* found is communion and hope.

PARTNERS OF THE 2014 VICTORIA STRAIT EXPEDITION

FEDERAL GOVERNMENT PARTNERS
Parks Canada
Royal Canadian Navy
Operation QIMMIQ
Canadian Coast Guard
Defence Research and Development Canada
Canadian Hydrographic Service
Canadian Space Agency
Canadian Ice Service
Government of Nunavut
Arctic Research Foundation
The Royal Canadian Geographical Society

ROYAL CANADIAN GEOGRAPHICAL SOCIETY PARTNERS
The W. Garfield Weston Foundation
One Ocean Expeditions
Shell Canada

NOTES

CHAPTER 2: TRIUMPHAL DEPARTURE

1. Quoted in Leslie H. Neatby, *Search for Franklin: The Story of One of the Great Dramas of Polar Exploration* (Edmonton: M.G. Hurtig, 1970), 84.

2. Quoted in Andrew D. Lambert, *Franklin: Tragic Hero of Polar Navigation* (London: Faber and Faber, 2009), 80.

3. Roderick Murchison, "Address to the Royal Geographical Society of London; Delivered at the Anniversary Meeting on the 26th May, 1945, by Roderick Impey Murchison, V.P.R.S. & G.S., Corr. Royal Inst. France, &c President," *Journal of the Royal Geographical Society* 15: xlvi.

4. Quoted in Lambert, *Franklin: Tragic Hero*, 165.

5. Quoted in Neatby, *Search for Franklin*, 13.

6. Ibid., 12–15.

7. John Franklin, *The Publications of the Champlain Society: Sir John Franklin's Journals and Correspondence: The First Arctic Land Expedition 1819–1822; Edited with an Introduction by Richard C. Davis*, ed. Robert Craig Brown (Toronto: Champlain Society, 1995), xxiii.

8. Jessica Richard, "'A Paradise of My Own Creation': Frankenstein and the Improbable Romance of Polar Exploration," *Nineteenth-Century Contexts* 25, no. 4 (2003): 304, doi:10.1080/08905490 32000167826; John Geiger and Owen Beattie, *Dead Silence: The Greatest Mystery in Arctic Discovery* (Toronto: Viking, 1993), 11.

9. Margaret Atwood, introduction, in Beattie and Geiger, *Frozen in Time: The Fate of the Franklin Expedition* (Vancouver: Greystone, 2014), 4.

10. Richard, "'A Paradise of My Own Creation,'" 300.

11. Owen Beattie and John Geiger, *Frozen in Time: The Fate of the Franklin Expedition* (Vancouver: Greystone, 2014), 45.

CHAPTER 3: DESPAIR

12. Quoted in Neatby, *Search for Franklin*, 267.

13. Ibid., 224.

CHAPTER 4: PRISONERS OF ICE

14. Quoted in David C. Woodman, *Unravelling the Franklin Mystery: Inuit Testimony* (Montreal: McGill-Queen's University Press, 1991), 198.

15. Ibid., 202.

16. Geiger and Beattie, *Dead Silence*, passim.

17. James P. Delgado, introduction, in *Narrative of a Journey to the Polar Sea in the Years 1819-20-21-22*, by John Franklin (Vancouver: Douglas & McIntyre, 2000), 19.

18. John Richardson, *Arctic Ordeal: The Journal of John Richardson, Surgeon-Naturalist with Franklin, 1820–1822*, ed. C. Stuart Houston (Montreal: McGill-Queen's University Press, 1994), ix.

19. Ibid.

20. Beattie and Geiger, *Frozen in Time*, 44.

21. Neatby, *Search for Franklin*, 73; Beattie and Geiger, *Frozen in Time*, 28–29.

22. Woodman, *Unravelling the Franklin Mystery*, 205–206.

23. Neatby, *Search for Franklin*, 98.

24. Francis Leopold McClintock, *In the Arctic Seas: A Narrative of the Discovery of the Fate of Sir John Franklin and His Companions* (Philadelphia: Porter & Coates, 1859), 267.

25. Francis Leopold McClintock, *The Voyage of the 'Fox' in the Arctic Seas: A Narrative of the Discovery of the Fate of Sir John Franklin and His Companions* (London: John Murray, 1859), 292.

26. Beattie and Geiger, *Frozen in Time*, 138–139.

CHAPTER 5: PRIDE

27. Michela Rosano, "The Maps: Seven Historical Charts Related to the Lost Franklin Expedition That Helped Shaped Canada's North," *Canadian Geographic*, December 2014, 82.

CHAPTER 6: MARCH OF DEATH

28. Michael Durey, "Exploration at the Edge: Reassessing the Fate of Sir John Franklin's Last Arctic Expedition," *The Great Circle* 30, no. 2 (2008): 5.

29. Quoted in Woodman, *Unravelling the Franklin Mystery*, 108.

30. Neatby, *Search for Franklin*, 118.

31. Admiralty medical journal, HMS *Enterprise*, 1848–49, ADM 101/99/4, National Archives (U.K.).

32. Ken McGoogan, *Lady Franklin's Revenge: A True Story of Ambition, Obsession and the Remaking of Arctic History* (Toronto: HarperCollins, 2005), 285.

33. Lambert, Franklin: *Tragic Hero*, 212.

34. Douglas R. Stenton, Anne Keenleyside and Robert W. Park, "The 'Boat Place' Burial: New Skeletal Evidence from the 1845 Franklin Expedition," *Arctic* 68, no. 1 (March 2015): 40–41, doi:10.14430/arctic4454.

35. Neatby, *Search for Franklin*, 245.

36. Beattie and Geiger, *Frozen in Time*, 116–117.

37. John Rae, "Dr. Rae's Letter to George Simpson," *The Albion: The British, Colonial, and Foreign Gazette*, October 28, 1854, www.ric.edu/faculty/rpotter/albion.html.

38. Quoted in Lambert, *Franklin: Tragic Hero*, 250.

39. McClintock, *Voyage of the 'Fox'*, 275.

40. Beattie and Geiger, *Frozen in Time*, 81.

41. McClintock, *Voyage of the 'Fox'*, 297.

42. Douglas R. Stenton, "A Most Inhospitable Coast: The Report of Lieutenant William Hobson's 1859 Search for the Franklin Expedition on King William Island," *Arctic* 67, no. 4 (December 2014): 518, doi:10.14430/arctic4424.

43. McClintock, *Voyage of the 'Fox'*, 296.

44. Lambert, *Franklin: Tragic Hero*, 283.

45. Woodman, *Unravelling the Franklin Mystery*, 209.

46. Ibid., 256.

EPILOGUE: THE AGE OF CHANGE

47. Margaret Atwood, *Strange Things: The Malevolent North in Canadian Literature* (Oxford: Clarendon Press, 1995), 17.

48. Ibid., 19.

49. Shelagh D. Grant, "How the Find Affects Canada's Case," *Canadian Geographic*, December 2014, 60.

50. Atwood, *Strange Things*, 28.

SELECTED BIBLIOGRAPHY

Atwood, Margaret. *Strange Things: The Malevolent North in Canadian Literature*. Oxford: Clarendon Press, 1995.

Beattie, Owen, and John Geiger. *Frozen in Time: The Fate of the Franklin Expedition*. Introduction by Margaret Atwood. Vancouver: Greystone, 2014.

Cawood, John. "The Magnetic Crusade: Science and Politics in Early Victorian Britain." *Isis*, 1979, 493–518.

Cohen, Andrew. *Lost Beneath the Ice: The Story of HMS* Investigator. Toronto: Dundurn, 2013.

Davis, Wade. *The Wayfinders: Why Ancient Wisdom Matters in the Modern World*. Toronto: House of Anansi Press, 2009.

Durey, Michael. "Exploration at the Edge: Reassessing the Fate of Sir John Franklin's Last Arctic Expedition." *The Great Circle* 30, no. 2 (2008): 3–40.

Eber, Dorothy. *Encounters on the Passage: Inuit Meet the Explorers*. Toronto: University of Toronto Press, 2008.

"A Franklin Find! The Real Inside Story of How *Erebus* Was Discovered." *Canadian Geographic*, December 2014, 1–98.

Franklin, John. *Narrative of a Journey to the Polar Sea in the Years 1819-20-21-22*. Introduction by James P. Delgado. Vancouver: Douglas & McIntyre, 2000.

———. *The Publications of the Champlain Society: Sir John Franklin's Journals and Correspondence: The First Arctic Land Expedition 1819–1822; Edited with an Introduction by Richard C. Davis*. Edited by Robert Craig Brown. Toronto: Champlain Society, 1995.

Geiger, John, and Owen Beattie. *Dead Silence: The Greatest Mystery in Arctic Discovery*. Toronto: Viking, 1993.

Good, Gregory A. "The Study of Geomagnetism in the Late 19th Century." *Eos, Transactions American Geophysical Union* 69, no. 16 (1988): 218–232.

Lambert, Andrew D. *Franklin: Tragic Hero of Polar Navigation*. London: Faber and Faber, 2009.

Larson, Edward J. *An Empire of Ice: Scott, Shackleton, and the Heroic Age of Antarctic Science*. New Haven: Yale University Press, 2011.

McClintock, Francis Leopold. *The Voyage of the 'Fox' in the Arctic Seas: A Narrative of the Discovery of the Fate of Sir John Franklin and His Companions*. London: John Murray, 1859.

McGoogan, Ken. *Fatal Passage: The Untold Story of John Rae, the Arctic Adventurer Who Discovered the Fate of Franklin*. Toronto: HarperFlamingo Canada, 2001.

———. *Lady Franklin's Revenge: A True Story of Ambition, Obsession and the Remaking of Arctic History*. Toronto: HarperCollins, 2005.

Neatby, Leslie H. *Search for Franklin: The Story of One of the Great Dramas of Polar Exploration.* Edmonton: M.G. Hurtig, 1970.

Rae, John. "Dr. Rae's Letter to George Simpson." *The Albion: The British, Colonial, and Foreign Gazette,* October 28, 1854. www.ric.edu/faculty/rpotter/albion.html.

Richard, Jessica. "'A Paradise of My Own Creation': Frankenstein and the Improbable Romance of Polar Exploration." *Nineteenth-Century Contexts* 25, no. 4 (2003): 295–314. doi:10.1080/0890549032000167826.

Richardson, John. *Arctic Ordeal: The Journal of John Richardson, Surgeon-Naturalist with Franklin, 1820–1822.* Edited by C. Stuart Houston. Montreal: McGill-Queen's University Press, 1994.

Sandler, Martin W. *Resolute: The Epic Search for the Northwest Passage and John Franklin, and the Discovery of the Queen's Ghost Ship.* New York: Sterling, 2006.

Shelley, Mary Wollstonecraft. *Frankenstein, or, The Modern Prometheus.* Edited by Maurice Hindle. London: Penguin Books, 2003.

Stenton, Douglas R. "A Most Inhospitable Coast: The Report of Lieutenant William Hobson's 1859 Search for the Franklin Expedition on King William Island." *Arctic* 67, no. 4 (December 2014): 511–522. doi:10.14430/arctic4424.

Stenton, Douglas R., Anne Keenleyside and Robert W. Park. "The 'Boat Place' Burial: New Skeletal Evidence from the 1845 Franklin Expedition." *Arctic* 68, no. 1 (March 2015): 32–44. doi:10.14430/arctic4454.

Woodman, David C. *Unravelling the Franklin Mystery: Inuit Testimony.* Montreal: McGill-Queen's University Press, 1991.

Zagon, Thomas. *Preliminary Analysis of Sea Ice Characteristics in Relation to the Lost Franklin Vessels HMS* Erebus *and HMS* Terror. Draft report. Canadian Ice Service, Meteorological Service of Canada, Environment Canada, 2011.